ROCKS IN MY SCOTCH

We told nobody about the hole in the wall or about what we had found behind it. Some years ago, in 1971, when the out-houses were being demolished before the arrival of a new minister, I made a special visit to see what was happening to the loft above the coal-house. It had already been demolished. In the yard lay heaps of rubble, with, here and there, what looked like pages of old books and magazines stuck in the midst of them, discoloured, forlorn, flapping in the wind.

I made no effort to identify them. I was still breaking into sealed lofts and learning about the world; but most of my eagerness and excitement had become diverted into less physical channels.

Angus MacVicar
Rocks in My Scotch

ARROW BOOKS

Arrow Books Limited
17–21 Conway Street, London W1P 6JD

An imprint of the Hutchinson Publishing Group

London Melbourne Sydney Auckland
Johannesburg and agencies
throughout the world

First published by Hutchinson 1977
Arrow edition 1982

© Angus MacVicar 1977

Set in Monotype Times New Roman

Made and printed in Great Britain
by The Anchor Press Ltd
Tiptree, Essex

ISBN 0 09 928101 8

To Willie, Kenneth and John
my brothers still, for a' that

Acknowledgements

In connection with the story about the Sollas evictions, my grateful thanks are due to John Prebble for allowing me to follow closely the line of his narrative in *The Highland Clearances*. I am grateful also to Captain Jack Broome for permission to use the story about the capture of a German spy which he tells in *Convoy is to Scatter*. For accurate information concerning the wrecks of the *Argo* and the *Dunraven Castle* I have to thank ex-Coxswain Duncan Newlands and the Royal National Lifeboat Institution.

A.M.

Contents

The Sealed Loft

It was in the late summer of 1919, when the excitements of the First World War were fading from a boy's short memory, that Archie and Willie and I solved the mystery of the sealed loft above the coal-house.

Archie was seven and Willie five. Rona, our sister, had been born – but only just – while brothers Kenneth and John had still to make their entrances. I was ten, a man of the world, far-travelled, having been to Campbeltown, ten miles away, several times and to Glasgow once.

The rigours of the journey to Campbeltown were considerable. It was by a motor-bus, an Oldsmobile of uncertain temper belonging to Mrs Gibson of the Argyll Arms Hotel, who persisted in calling it, with hazy topicality, the 'Demobilize'. The driver was her nephew, Willie McKerral, whose sister Jean, then only nine years old, I was eventually to marry.

The 'Demobilize' was uncovered. Passengers had to sit side by side on long benches, facing in towards each other like actors in a classic Russian film, unsheltered from rain, sun or tempest. It shuddered and shook along the metalled road, occasionally suffered broken springs and punctures and, when faced by Kilellan Brae (with a full load and the wind against), began to bubble, boil and whine, with the result that old farmers with cloth caps, oilskin coats, well-trimmed whiskers and rose-brier pipes, along with young women and children like my mother and myself, had to get out and walk alongside as it struggled to the top. Today, even in my eight-year-old Morris Oxford, I can surge up and over Kilellan Brae in top gear and scarcely notice it.

On the journey to Glasgow further hazards had to be faced in the *Davaar* or the *Kinloch*, the elegant steamers which ran daily from Campbeltown to Gourock, via Carradale and Lochranza. Even for me, sophisticated traveller though I was, the sight of white-caps in Kilbrannan Sound and of watery turbulence off the Garroch Head were daunting. Queasiness occurred in my stomach, not from seasickness but from anxiety. I comforted myself by remembering a tale often told by my seafaring friend, old Hughie Stewart. Seated on a bollard on the ancient stone jetty under the Rock of Dunaverty, Hughie would pause in the manufacture of lobster creels and describe to us boys, held fast by his 'glittering eye', how, from the deck of the *Kinloch* in Kilbrannan Sound, he had once seen a passing ship raised so high by waves at bow and stern that under her hull he had glimpsed the rocky coastline of Kintyre! I was grateful that conditions on my journey were scarcely as terrible as that.

But, as I afterwards informed my goggling brothers, the supreme test of my discipline and courage occurred on the train which carried us from Gourock to Glasgow. Scarcely had I recovered from the heart-stopping trauma of plunging un-expectedly into a dark tunnel when another train approached with a howl and a roar and, as I thought, almost collided with us. I sat zombiefied as it screamed past, apparently missing us only by inches. The danger receded. I opened my eyes, took a deep breath and – to prove hardihood – remarked to my mother, 'Great drivers in these trains!'

Not only did I venture in public transport: I also rode a bicycle, an important status symbol in a parish where people – even farmers – were then generally poor, with children lucky to own boots, let alone bicycles. On it, during the summer holidays, I explored roads and glens and practised dirt-track riding on the beaches and on the gravelled Manse drive. It was a sturdy second-hand model bought for a pound from my school pal, Bobby Kelly, a nephew of red-bearded Hugh McEachran who was my father's Kirk Treasurer. The same Bobby is now himself

Kirk Treasurer (and still a pal), which shows that family tradi-
tions flourish strongly in a small community like Southend at
the Mull of Kintyre.

By 1919 my father had been minister of Southend for nine
years. One of those years, from 1916 to 1917, he had spent in
Greece as a chaplain attached to the Lovat Scouts, which is
why he came to be known as the Padre. He and my mother,
along with ourselves and Maimie, the sentimental, kind but
hard-knuckled little maid, occupied a three-storeyed Manse
with nine rooms, a bathroom, a scullery and a large collection
of out-houses.

The out-houses included a garden shed *cum* earthen closet at
the back, with, in front, between the Manse and the main road,
a complex of buildings comprising a hen-house, a washing-
house, a stable, a barn, a byre and a coal-house.

There was also, by itself near the front gate, a dark, dank
structure which we called 'Peter's Shed', after a neighbouring
farmer who used it for storing his reapers, ploughs, grubbers and
other agricultural implements. Though no person or document
can be found to confirm it, I believe this building to have been
the old Manse ('rendered excessively damp by two great trees
which overshadow it and suffering from the effects of fire',
according to a chronicler of the period), left derelict when the
new Manse in which we lived was built in 1818.

All those out-houses were relics of an era when a Church of
Scotland clergyman was also a farmer and cultivated the
Church glebelands for his own profit, though long before my
father came to Southend the glebelands had been rented out to
Peter Galbraith (who gave his name to 'Peter's Shed') and most
of them were redundant as far as a minister was concerned.
Sometimes, however, the byre was used by farmers as a shelter
for cattle being driven to and from the market in Campbeltown;
and the stable came in handy for churchgoers and visitors to
the Manse, most of whom travelled in horse-drawn 'machines'.

At the time, indeed, only one private motor-car existed in
Southend – apart from the Dowager Duchess of Argyll's

Daimler, with its studded tyres and uniformed chauffeur. It belonged to one of my father's leading elders, James Hunter of Machribeg Farm, and we regarded it with the awe reserved by schoolboys today for a flying saucer. It rattled on speedy but erratic courses throughout Kintyre. Hens scattered from its path, squawking. In the fields large Clydesdale horses heard it coming, reared, neighed and fled thunderously to far corners. As it hurtled past the school at thirty miles an hour we would rush to climb the high playground wall and, from this safe eminence, cheer its progress.

Stories regarding Jamie Hunter's driving thrilled and delighted us.

Once he reversed into the window of a china-shop in Campbeltown with smashing results. Another time, attempting a dashing U-turn, he destroyed a wooden hen-house in his own backyard and declared afterwards that it hadn't been there in the morning when he left. Directly opposite the junction of Machribeg farm-track with the main road, there is a gateway into a field. One morning, no doubt preoccupied with thoughts concerning milk-yields and turnip crops, he failed to make the turn on to the highway and plunged straight across it and through the gateway into a slough of cattle-churned mud. The motor coughed itself to death. He banged the steering-wheel. 'Who left that dashed gate open!' he complained.

It was James Hunter who first greeted my father on his arrival by steamer at Campbeltown in March 1910 and drove him, my mother, Maimie and me eight miles south to our new home in the Manse of St Blaan. He used a 'machine': his car had not then been purchased. And it was Jamie Hunter who conveyed our furniture from the pier – in long, ladder-sided carts – and organized help among his fellow-farmers to unload and instal it.

His kindness to 'the minister' and to the minister's family never varied throughout his life. After the First World War, when he exchanged his pony and 'machine' for the car, he continued to offer my father 'lifts' to Campbeltown and beyond. Not wishing to hurt a loyal elder and friend my father had to accept a few such invitations; but my mother, brothers, Maimie and I – though willing enough – were never allowed to accompany him. 'One member of the family risking his life is enough,' he used to say.

His most anguished experience, he often told us, was on a return journey from Campbeltown to Southend, in a fog. On Kilellan Brae (which runs downhill in this direction) the fog was so dense that Jamie ordered my father to put his head out of the passenger window and keep a sharp look-out, while he did the same on *his* side. The road was being remetalled and, following custom, small piles of stones had been deposited at close intervals along the verge, ready for scattering. Suddenly the car's near-wheels bumped over one of those and then, in quick succession, over another and another.

'Broken a spring!' shouted the driver, to whom such accidents were not unknown.

'You haven't!' my father shouted back. 'You're bumping on the road metal!'

'No road metal here!'

'Yes, there is! Steer away from it!'

'If I steer away from it I'll hit the other side!'

'Isn't there plenty of room?'

'How do I know, minister! I can't see!'

The crashing and bumping continued. Bones jarring, my father prayed. Near the foot of the hill the piles of road metal came to an end and the fog cleared.

'I told you!' cried Jamie, almost hysterical with relief. 'There's no road metal here. These dashed springs!'

The Padre, breathing heavily, made no further comment.

He seldom took a dram at home. That night he did. I remember him saying to my mother: 'Greater love hath no man than this, that he lay down his life for Jamie Hunter!'

All the same, he – and all of us – loved Jamie Hunter. He had known tragedy in the death of an adolescent son; but bitterness was never allowed to darken his hopeful spirit.

The derelict out-houses at the Manse might have been of little use to a non-farming minister; to a minister's sons they were caves of exciting romance.

An exception was the barn, a high, airy building used by my father as a kind of timber-yard. When trees were felled in the Manse grounds, or branches blown off by a roistering wind from the west, they were stored in the barn for sawing and chopping into firewood. My brothers and I were forbidden to wield the big axe, in case we did ourselves an injury; but from about the age of nine I had to take a turn at helping the Padre with the cross-cut saw. This, for me, was purgatory.

The preliminaries were always happy enough. Under paternal direction Archie and Willie and I would manoeuvre the sawing-horse into position and, with much tugging and heaving, lift the branch on to it. Having learned from experience, Archie and Willie would then stand back, well clear of trouble. My smiling father would take off his jacket, suddenly appearing oddly naked in dog-collar, shirt-sleeves and braces, and say to me: 'Come on now, Angus. See how many blocks we can make before tea!'

He would place the blade of the saw across the branch, the narrow end in my direction. 'Catch!' he'd say, in high good humour. I'd catch the wooden handle as instructed, but from my heart humour would be absent. At the beginning of operations such as sawing, gardening or repairing punctures on bicycles the Padre was invariably happy and carefree. It was later on, when things went sour, that hell might be glimpsed beneath the gates of heaven.

He had an impatient and somewhat irascible nature. One afternoon it happened that the branch we were sawing was young, sappy and tough, and the cross-cut needed sharpening. Each time it stuck he became more annoyed, his wrenching and pushing more savage. I teetered and staggered, trying to lend assistance. My puny efforts were not appreciated. The branch, the saw and I were denigrated in turn, terrible unministerial words issuing from behind clenched teeth. Archie and Willie giggled in the shadows.

At last the saw became so firmly embedded that even my father's frenzied jerks could not move it. He flung up his hands. 'Useless!' he roared at me. 'Useless!' he roared at the saw. Then he drew back a foot and kicked the horse with such force that along with branch and twanging saw it crashed over on its side. At the same moment he uttered a cry of pain and began hopping on one leg, nursing a bruised foot in both hands.

Archie and Willie fled outside, like camp followers from Culloden. As the eldest son I felt it was my duty to stay with my stricken father and, for want of anything better to do, make feeble efforts to raise the horse.

'Let it lie!' keened the Padre, collapsing on a pile of wood. 'Let the blasted thing lie!'

I departed the scene. Collecting my brothers from beneath the gooseberry bushes in the garden (a favourite hiding-place in times of stress), I led them into the hills behind the Manse. By tea-time, as I well knew, my father's passion would be spent and life would have returned to normal. In the meantime we could search, maybe with profit, for peewits' eggs.

Fifty years later, when the Padre was almost ninety, he was in Achnamara, our bungalow in Southend, watching on television a football match between Scotland and Germany. At the turn of the century as a Glasgow University student, he himself had played shinty for Scotland, and ever since had been interested in sport of all kinds. This day, according to him, the Germans were 'savages', kicking the Scots and getting away with it because of 'that blasted referee'. Kenneth Wolstenholme's commentary also enraged him. 'An Englishman supporting the Germans!' he snarled. 'No wonder there's a Scottish Nationalist Party!'

Suddenly, in full view of the cameras, a player was scythed down in a particularly vicious tackle. The victim writhed in agony – as soccer players, those fugitives from amateur drama, are frequently inclined to do. 'There you are!' exclaimed the ninety-year-old, throwing himself back in his armchair. 'They're at it again! That poor Scots boy!'

'But it's a German who's down,' Jean told him.

'Eh?' He peered forward to confirm the fact. 'So it is!' he declared with satisfaction. 'Let him lie!'

The Padre could never have been described as unprejudiced or even fair-minded. And yet, as we grew older, it was revealed to Rona, my brothers and me that he was a good minister.

All kinds of people – 'tinkers, tailors, soldiers, sailors, dons and duchesses and dukes', but mainly, in a country community like Southend, farmers and farm-workers – called regularly at the Manse for advice. Sometimes his advice was curt, if it concerned a material problem; but when men and women came to him weeping in despair he often wept with them, the quick tears of a Hebridean heritage staining his cheeks as he called for my mother to bring cups of tea.

He visited his congregation with tireless zeal, riding the rough roads on his bicycle and ignoring the weather. He made humorous speeches at weddings. With my mother he would often be the first visitor to touch the hand of a new-born child. When a parishioner was ill he would sit for hours by the bed-side; and when death became imminent he would be there to say a prayer for the dying, followed by another to support and comfort the living.

He always worked hard in preparing for a funeral. Once, to a young minister, I heard him give this advice: 'Always be at your best at a funeral, because at a funeral you get nearest to the hearts of your people.' His belief was that a minister had to be close to members of his congregation – a part, indeed, of their daily lives – in order to be of any spiritual use to them.

At the beginning we imagined he was far kinder and more tolerant with parishioners than he was with us. When sawing-horses were kicked with violence and bicycles which resisted his efforts at repair were thrown over the bank beyond the back gate, we often wondered what had happened to the benign approach he seemed to reserve for drunk men and for girls who were going to have illegitimate babies. Later on we realized that only in the superficial, unimportant areas of life did the Padre tend to blow gaskets. When serious moral problems were involved he could understand and sympathize, perhaps because he had personal experience of them.

The sealed loft was above the coal-house, the only means of access to it being a wooden door high on one wall of the barn. Since our arrival at the Manse this door had remained locked, with three stout planks nailed across it. As far as we could discover there was no key.

Archie, Willie and I were constantly curious about what lay behind it.

Maimie would say: 'I am sure *I* can't tell you! It's none of my business, nor of yours either. *Chiall beannachd mi*, there are more important things to worry about than a dirty old loft. I shouldn't be surprised if there's nothing at all inside.'

'If there's nothing inside why is it nailed up?'

'To keep inquisitive boys like you out of mischief – and to save you from breaking your necks trying to climb up to it. Now, skedaddle! Let me get on with making the dinner.'

'But, Maimie' – Archie was persistent – 'maybe there's a ghost in there?'

'Merciful goodness, if there *is* a ghost, you'd be wise to leave it alone, safely locked up. So stop asking questions! Outside you go and get some fresh air. Ghosts! Lord preserve us!'

But we knew that by his mention of a ghost Archie had touched a sensitive string in the constantly twanging harp of Maimie's personality. Born in Perthshire, the home of the Picts and the pixies, she had been brought up in a climate of superstition; and, as a legacy from my father's first parish, she had carried with her to Southend some spine-chilling yarns. One of those was about the Maid of Glen Duror, an apparition which, while prowling in the dark, would seem to have lit up like the phosphorescent tree-stump outside the Manse front gate. The idea that another 'Maid' might exist in the loft above the coal-house had obviously occurred to her as well as to Archie; and, despite the brusque manner in which duty prompted her to deal with us, we felt we might have gained a secret ally in our campaign to get that door opened.

My mother parried questions with patience and common sense. She was of farming stock from Appin, a nursery that has always produced more practical and down-to-earth characters than Perthshire, Maimie's homeland, or than North Uist, my father's.

'It was sealed up before we came,' she said. 'Seems that when the Manse was being got ready for us, nine years ago, they threw a lot of old rubbish up there and decided simply to lock it away. At least, so Mr Hunter tells us. There's no key, as far as I know.'

It sounded reasonable.

'What kind of rubbish?' I asked.

'How should I know? Now, don't bother your heads about it any more. There are far more exciting and interesting things to do outside. You haven't caught any tadpoles lately. Here's an old glass jelly-jar. How about trying to find some up at the Carr Loch?'

The diversion was maternally cunning. It was also successful. Tadpoles *were* exciting and, once caught, might turn into frogs before our very eyes. But on this occasion, when they died instead – the glass jar, though full of water and nourishing weed, being, because of our ignorance, without any kind of aeration – our minds returned to the burr-like problem of the loft.

The subject was never fully discussed with the Padre. If one of us dared to mention it he would snort down his nose – with the strong, curling red hairs sticking out of the nostrils – and tell us to mind our own blasted business. 'Away you go now and practise jump, hop and step or something!' (He had spoken nothing but Gaelic until he went to school in North Uist at the age of five. Ever since then he had been troubled by the English idiom. As he himself used to joke, unwittingly, he was always 'putting the horse before the cart'.)

In time our frustration led to an inevitable conclusion. By some means we ourselves must find a way into the loft.

Years later Archie became a teacher of English, Willie a ship's captain, I myself a spinner of tales. The way we approached our problem indicates that we mistook our vocations. We ought to have joined the secret service, or, perhaps, become demolition experts.

From the beginning we recognized that a direct assault on the door, high on the barn wall, was out of the question. Long before we could remove all the planks and force the lock, the operation was bound to be discovered. The barn, as well as being open to the back yard, was often entered by Maimie when collecting logs for the fire and by the Padre when he came to split them. Besides, if we were caught 'damaging property', as my Tory mother liked to phrase it, then the punishment would be dire, a heavy price to pay even for satisfied curiosity. A way of entry, therefore, must be found elsewhere.

At the age of five, Willie already had a navigator's imagination and sense of direction. Casually he suggested that we might try to force an entrance through the wall directly *opposite* the door in the barn. This, he said, could be done in secret from the adjacent loft above the byre, the door to which loomed twelve feet up on an outside gable wall near the back gate.

It was a brilliant idea, and Archie and I became convinced immediately that we had thought of it ourselves. The loft above the byre was already a 'gang headquarters', where on wet days we and other boys in the parish got together to consume secret hoards of liquorice straps and sometimes to wield them violently in dispensing summary justice to erring members of our fraternity. Our parents and Maimie never objected to our use of the household steps to reach the door, though sometimes they made noises of protest when the older ones among us, fired by tales of Everest in the *Boys' Own Paper*, indulged in the practice of hauling up on ropes some of the infants like Willie, who could not quite stretch up to the threshold from the top of the steps. We were lucky to have a childhood uninhibited by physical mollycoddling and, as will be shown, in a moral sense the story was similar. It seemed evident to us, therefore, that visits to the loft above the byre would cause no suspicion and that we might even be able to enter the loft above the coal-house and discover its contents without anybody being the wiser.

One Saturday morning, with rain spattering on a chill wind from the east, we asked Maimie politely if we could have the steps. On receiving her permission, we placed them in position below the outside door of the loft above the byre. From the Padre's incoherent tool-kit in the barn I took a hammer and chisel and secured them with string underneath my jersey. I climbed up, got inside the loft and helped Archie and Willie, suitably roped like mountaineers, in their scramble to join me.

We made a recce of the blank face of stone and mortar which was all that separated us from the sealed loft above the coal-house. The mortar was old and flaking. At one place we found a group of stones from which some had fallen away. Taking turns, we began work with the hammer and chisel to remove more.

The German prison camp at Colditz was still twenty years in the future; a television series was utterly beyond our reckoning. But we were not without ideas. We shut the loft door in order to muffle sounds and hammered and chiselled in the dark, using only a battery torch which had been a Christmas present to Archie from the Dowager Duchess. The mortar debris we placed in a bag – an old jelly-straining bag abandoned some time ago by my mother on a back shelf of the larder – and, at intervals, emptied it out of sight beneath a pile of straw in a corner.

On that first spell, though we laboured tensely until it was time for lunch, we failed to loosen any of the stones. It was a disappointment; but we were confident that another hour or two of work would bring us to the edge of triumph.

Unfortunately, the day was a Saturday. In the afternoon we

had to attend a children's party at a neighbouring farm. On Sunday, on account of holy observances, a visit to the loft would be impossible. On Monday we had to return to school after the summer holidays. Our first chance to resume operations, therefore, would not occur until the Monday evening.

We spent the week-end in a state of anxiety, even though the home-baked iced cakes and sliced sugared oranges at the farm party – and the moment in church, when to everyone's horror and secret delight, the Padre announced his text from *Galatians*: 'But now, after ye have known God, or rather are known of God, how turn ye again to the weak and buggarly elements' – helped in some measure to ease the burden.

A diversion took place on the Monday morning. It was to be Willie's first day at school, and it soon became evident that going to school was the last thing Willie wanted to do. Perhaps he had visions of working in the loft by himself while Archie and I were busy at our lessons. In any case, when the time came for the Padre to convoy us the short half-mile to Southend Public School, whose headmaster was the blond and bristling Mr James Inglis Morton, he was nowhere to be found.

We searched the dining-room, the drawing-room, the attics, the bedrooms: no sign of him. My mother struggled to camouflage tears. Scuttling about in all directions, Maimie let loose imprecations in the Gaelic, imprecations directed not at Willie but at the Padre for his angry shouts. Archie and I were beginning to be afraid that we might be late for school, which would mean the strap. Mr Morton accepted no excuses, not even from parents.

From above there was a faint sound. Archie and I raced upstairs. In the spare bedroom we discovered Willie below the big double bed, cowering beyond our reach against a corner of the wall.

'Come on,' said Archie, 'we'll be late!'

'I don't want to go to school!'

'Don't be stupid!' I said, in a low voice. 'If the Padre finds you in there he'll kill you!'

'I don't want to go to school!'

I went hurriedly downstairs and got my father's long *cromak* from the hallstand. In the kitchen, upset by the commotion, Rona was howling in her pram, being comforted by our distraught mother.

'Have you found him yet?' bellowed the Padre, rummaging in the rhododendrons at the front door.

I didn't answer.

Half-way up the stairs I met Maimie coming down. She eyed the *cromak*.

'You've found him?'

'Don't tell anybody!' I said.

'The poor dear child – hunted like an animal! You should all think black burning shame of yourselves!'

Black burning shame was something of which – as yet – I had small experience; and, in any case, it was clear that Maimie had no alternative plans to offer. I got down on my knees by the bed and poked at Willie.

'Buck up! You're not a baby any longer!'

For a time he suffered the pokes in miserable silence. Archie pled with him, even promising the gift of a whole liquorice strap if only he'd come out.

Willie said: 'I don't want to go to school!'

I began to make long sweeps with the *cromak*. As it struck Willie's legs I felt cruel and guilty. But in the end the new assault proved effective. He crawled out, uttering heavy sobs.

We led him downstairs. 'It's all right,' I told the Padre, whose complexion had become ruddier than I'd ever seen it before. 'He's coming now.'

In a great silence we trudged down the road to the school – the Padre, Archie, Willie and I. We weren't late. Willie's scholastic career began in an atmosphere of sadness and twanging, ill-received discipline.

His next rebellion occurred when he was sixteen, a pupil at Campbeltown Grammar School. Suddenly he announced that he had had enough of conventional education and was going to join the merchant navy. Long afterwards, as senior Captain with the Anchor Line, he himself brooked no soft options among his apprentices. When appointed to his ship they groaned in concert and hastened to get their hair cut.

But on the evening of that first day of Willie's schooling, before we went to work again in the loft above the byre, I happened to approach the window of the study, where I saw and overheard my father and mother talking inside. They spoke quietly. To my astonishment I detected tears in my father's eyes and voice.

'Poor wee soul,' he was saying. 'I can never get used to this terrible first day at school.'

'Neither can I.' My mother's mouth was awry. 'It's heart-rending.'

'It seems all wrong that we should always have to appear hard and unsympathetic. But I suppose it's for their own good in the end.'

I went thoughtfully to Maimie to borrow the steps.

An hour later I had emotional problems of my own. So had Archie and Willie, and the morning's traumatic events were temporarily forgotten. A large stone moved as I twisted with the chisel. It fell away from us into the loft above the coal-house, dustily dragging with it smaller stones on either side. Silent on a peak, not in Darien but in a Manse out-house, we glimpsed the unknown.

The unknown, from our position, appeared to be an empty wooden floor.

I was shaking. In my imagination living creatures lurked in the dark, just out of sight: rats, voles, perhaps even animals about which we knew nothing, like the prehistoric monsters found in a secret cave in Egypt, as described by Captain Charles H. Gilson in his current *BOP* serial. But I was the eldest. Archie and Willie were looking at me: I was the experienced one, the far-travelled sophisticate.

This is the burden of being the eldest. You are an innovation, the object of experiments by apprentice parents. You are expected, on account of seniority, to be an experimenter and innovator yourself, with curious eyes constantly watching how you go. All my life I have hated this role; but all my life I have played it to the best of my ability, as a kind of challenge to a weakness in my character. I suppose it was an important motivation in my becoming a writer. It certainly causes bitter self-denigration and intermittent stomach ulcers – that is, when experiments go wrong and innovations fail. When they succeed, I believe it causes the euphoric vainglory which also afflicts me.

While Archie and Willie waited, I accepted the situation with much the same fatalism as later on I came to know more intimately before leaving home for the university, before joining the army, before leading a platoon ashore on Madagascar, before my first television broadcast.

I said, like a character in a low-budget Western: 'Come on, let's go!'

I pushed and scraped and wrestled a way through the hole, landing on my elbows on the bare floor. Archie came next with the torch. We dragged Willie in beside us.

We stood still, daunted now by silence, while Archie directed light around and into every corner of the loft. No rat stirred. No monster reared or snarled.

There was nothing in the loft except what looked like a pile of rubbish in one corner. The sense of danger passed. Powerful curiosity reasserted itself.

We approached the pile and saw that it consisted mainly of mouldering books, magazines, papers – and empty medicine bottles. There were scores of bottles, most of them of purple corrugated glass. (Not long ago I saw similar ones for sale in a Glasgow antique shop at 40p each.)

I was interested in the books and magazines.

A number of the books were collections of sermons by somebody called Spurgeon. Born of a confusion of ill-digested facts culled from Arthur Mee's *Children's Newspaper*, I had a vision

of a fish-headed man curved over a desk, regularly dipping his
pen in caviare.

But then, while Archie and Willie scrabbled in the pile for
more bottles – they would make excellent targets for stone-
throwing practice down in the glebe – I commandeered the
torch and began to look through the magazines. Presently it
occurred to me that in their damp pages I had discovered the
secret of the sealed loft.

Some of the magazines, including about a dozen copies of
Chambers's Journal dated 1906 and 1907, were not illustrated
and so, to my untutored eye, appeared uninteresting. They had
advertisements, however, which *were* illustrated; and one of
those, for a sparse moment, held my attention. It was headed
FREQUENT MICTURITION. Below this intriguing phrase – and
above some letterpress and an announcement of price – was a
drawing of something like a bag, with straps attached, which
defied my comprehension. I had a feeling of inadequacy. Here
was I, ten years old and, as I thought, full of knowledge. Here
also, staring at me from a slimy page, were a word and an
illustration at the meaning of which I could not even guess. The
world and my future life in it began to threaten more worries
than ever they had done before.

I pushed the *Chambers's Journals* aside and began to look at
a set of magazines printed on thick art paper. Those, I found –
in a publisher's phrase learned in later years – were 'lavishly
illustrated'.

A few of the pictures were signed by an artist whose name I
made out to be Aubrey Beardsley. To me they were grotesque,
unreal, infinitely disagreeable. Aubrey Beardsley had created
men and women outside my experience, hobgoblins who would
mock and terrify me if, one day, I should be forced to meet them
in the flesh in a world beyond Southend.

Other pictures, unsigned, were even more frightening. One
showed a bearded man holding a flimsily dressed young girl in a
savage embrace. Another showed a creature with cloven hooves
playing what might have been a gigantic mouth-organ, while,

near by, a naked man fondled a naked woman beneath a tree. Yet another showed a voluptuous lady reclining on a bed. She was gazing up at the ceiling, where – of all things – a swan was hovering in a kind of cloud.

As I turned the pages with hands which had begun to tremble, I saw more in the same style. Excitingly pleasant thrills invaded my body. My mouth became dry. I wished I had been alone, without responsibility for Archie and Willie.

I felt then what I think Adam must have felt when he smiled at Eve and took the first bite of the apple. Where innocence had been before, now there was a stirring of lusty male awareness, a recognition of the need to camouflage pleasurable feeling in a society with guilt-ridden rules concerning behaviour. This was an end – or a beginning.

I rearranged the pile, so that the art magazines were hidden underneath the books and the bottles. I said to Archie and Willie: 'Nothing interesting here. Take some of the bottles for plunking at. Come on.'

Archie said: 'What were those pictures you got so interested in?'

'Oh, just rubbish. Landscapes and such like.' It was the first lie I had ever told him.

We retrieved the hammer and chisel and squirmed through the hole, back to the loft above the byre. Puffing and groaning we manoeuvred the stones back into the wall. I lowered Archie and Willie down to the steps, then shut the loft door behind me.

In the yard we met Maimie. 'Merciful goodness, the state of your clothes! What on earth have you been doing?'

'Playing in the loft.'

'Go to the bathroom at once and get cleaned up before your parents see you!'

We obeyed. Her eyes were suspicious as she looked after us. But she kept her suspicions to herself.

On the previous day I would almost certainly have asked her about 'micturition'. Now things had changed. But before going to bed that night, taking care to let nobody see me, I looked up the word in *Chambers's Twentieth Century Dictionary*, which had a prominent place in the Padre's big bookcase. What I found made a life which loomed ahead even more complicated and strange.

We told nobody about the hole in the wall or about what we had found behind it. Some years ago, in 1971, when the out-houses were being demolished before the arrival of a new minister, I made a special visit to see what was happening to the loft above the coal-house. It had already been demolished. In the yard lay heaps of rubble, with, here and there, what looked like pages of old books and magazines stuck in the midst of them, discoloured, forlorn, flapping in the wind.

I made no effort to identify them. I was still breaking into sealed lofts and learning about the world; but most of my eagerness and excitement had become diverted into less physical channels.

2

The Irish Connection

Archie, Willie and I were all born before the First World War. Rona, our only sister, was born in 1918, Kenneth in 1921 and John, the youngest, in 1927, when my mother was in her forty-eighth year.

In July 1943, while serving as an officer with the Argylls in the Second World War, Archie was fatally wounded by a German mortar shell during the battle for Gerbini in Sicily. He was an Honours Graduate in English, a teacher at Dunoon Grammar School. Rona was also a teacher, in Campbeltown. In September 1949, less than a year after winning the Gold Medal for solo singing at the Gaelic Mod in Glasgow, she died of cancer.

There is a small Celtic cross to their memory in Keil-colm-cille, the graveyard in Southend. It bears an inscription, 'They were lovely and pleasant in their lives.' I can vouch for its truth. Even after so many years, their blond good looks, their patient gallantry, their disciplined eagerness for life can still, for me, buttress spells of unhappiness.

Willie, Kenneth and John remain alive.

After thirty-five years as a sea captain Willie has retired. His first command was a ship's life-boat containing eighty-two survivors when the 9000-ton liner *Britannia*, under charter to the Ministry of War Transport, was sunk by a German raider off the west coast of Africa on 25 March 1941. The desperate journey ended on the island of Corupu, near San Luiz de Maranhão in Brazil, on 16 April. Willie still can't swim, but I am told that his officers and men were never loath to go to sea with him.

Kenneth has been minister of Kenmore in Perthshire since 1950. Like Willie, he also had trouble during the Second World War, when his reconnaissance Hurricane was shot down over Kinbin, north of the Chindwin, on 22 December 1944. He spent a week in the jungle, being harried and shot at by the Japanese, until at last he stumbled into the welcoming arms of a platoon of Gordon Highlanders. His parishioners in Kenmore – and the people of Loch Tayside in general – look upon him with mingled affection and alarm. Like his father, he is a good minister, inclined on occasion to be irascible, authoritarian and un-orthodox. But as he understands his people, so they understand him. This is the best testimonial that can possibly be given to a clergyman.

At the age of forty-nine, John is a mere child compared with the rest of us. He is now Professor of Midwifery at the University of Leicester, with so many medical degrees after his name that my unacademic mind fairly boggles at the sight of them. His status as a good doctor, however, may better be measured, I believe, by the remarkable number of children he has brought into the world who have been given his name.

Except for the final and perhaps the most important one, Willie, Kenneth, John and I have opened a great many more sealed lofts than Archie and Rona did in their short lives. But we count ourselves lucky that as we open lofts we are able to judge their contents against a background of faith instilled in us by our parents, by precept and example – a faith which we later tried and tested for ourselves and have never found wanting.

We are also privileged in that we grew up in an atmosphere of 'family', which taught us a recognition of the rights of others, and in that we have roots in the parish of Southend, which, even yet, has not been too much affected by the modern disease of 'material sophistication'.

In Southend we can, I think, recognize our true inheritance. A Scottish inheritance which, in the first place, came from Celtic Ireland.

My study window looks out across the blue flats of the

North Channel. In September, when a north wind blows, I can
see on the other side Red Bay's enclosing arms, Garron's Point
and Rownabay Head, and, using binoculars, may catch a
glimpse of work going on in the high harvest fields. In the background I recognize my constant companions, the round hills of
Antrim, which look to me like fairy hills in a Walt Disney
cartoon.

From our bungalow, here on the south coast of Southend, the
distance to Rownabay Head is approximately seventeen miles.
In the *Proceedings of the Royal Irish Academy* (Vol. VIII)
Dr Reeves has this to say about my parish: 'The whole district
is strongly impressed with social and ecclesiastical features of
an Irish character. . . . The traditional associations of the
people all look westward, and the titles of nearly all the adjacent
parishes are commemorative of illustrious worthies of the
Irish Church.'

Southend is a natural pier-head for Irish visitors; and ever
since the arrival in Kintyre of the first mesolithic men from
Ireland, around 8000 years ago, there has always been a
coming – and a going, too – across the narrow sea.

Here, in the early ages, there landed the *Scotti*, the Irish tribe
which gave its name to Scotland. Here, in AD 563, there landed
Columba, the saint who gave us Christianity – the greatest
saint of them all, in my opinion, because his halo, though
shining with the Spirit, was also jaunty and even a little crooked.

Here there landed noble lords from Erin with their soldiers,
armourers and sennachies (or story-tellers). Here there landed
fishermen and farmers from Antrim seeking new and perhaps
more lucrative employment – and also William Burke, on his
way to body-snatching ploys with William Hare in Edinburgh.
Here there landed smugglers, potato-gatherers, thatchers,
peddlars of linen goods, whose names and deeds, all of Irish
origin, are commemorated in the songs called 'Come-all-ye's'
still sung at our local concerts. From here, during the Second
World War, there sailed a German spy bearing news of a convoy
to his German friends in the Irish Free State.

Here, today, from boats on a summer jaunt, there land men from the Walt Disney hills – men with names like McCambridge and McNeill who come among us to exchange knowledge of past and present and to invite us across to sample the hospitality of the Glynns. Here, not long ago, there landed pupils from an Antrim school who came to meet the children of Southend and make a radio programme. All were wary of each other, suspecting different looks and accents, until somebody mentioned Rangers and Celtic. Then the arguments and the friendships grew.

Two 'monuments' in Southend typify the close affinity between Kintyre and Antrim. The Padre was never too busy to show them off to visitors. Now I have taken his place as an unofficial local 'guide'.

The first is a flat rock above the churchyard at Keil, less than a mile away from Achnamara. On it are carved the prints of two right feet, known to us as 'St Columba's Footsteps'.

I believe the prints were there long before Columba's time; and, indeed, the Royal Commission on the Ancient and Historical Monuments of Scotland shares this opinion, estimating that the one nearer the sea, aligned east and west, is some 3000 years old. Here, I am convinced, is yet another example of the 'fealty foot' once used by a newly elected chief when swearing faithfulness to his tribe.

The custom, born in antiquity, was still being followed by the Clan Donald as late as the fourteenth century; and a MacDonald sennachie has handed down the following description of the ceremony of proclaiming the Lords of the Isles: 'The Bishop of Argyle, the Bishop of the Isles and seven priests were sometimes present with the chieftains of the principal families. There was a square stone seven or eight feet long and the tract of a man's foot cut thereon upon which the ruler of the Isles stood, denoting that he should walk in the footsteps and uprightness of his predecessors, and that he was installed by right in his possessions. He was clothed in a white habit to show that he would be a light to his people and maintain the true religion.

Then he received a white rod in his hand, intimating that he had power to rule not with tyranny and particularity but with discretion and sincerity. Next he was given his forefather's sword or some other sword, signifying that his duty was to protect and defend his people.'

Though the 'fealty foot' was carved in the rock at Keil before his coming, imagination can picture Columba – an astute statesman as well as a churchman – taking his stand in the footprint (or footprints), first facing the east and the rising sun like a new chief, then turning northward to address the people gathered on the steep hillside, a hillside known in Gaelic to this day as *guala na popuill*, 'the shoulder of the congregation'.

Our second 'monument' with an Irish connection is the Rock of Dunaverty. Like the Antrim hills, I can see it from my window half a mile distant across Machribeg Bay, a lump of Old Red Sandstone, ninety feet high. It once boasted a MacDonald Castle, the fighting part on the Rock itself, the living quarters for families and camp-followers on the high dune on its eastern flank. In the *New Statistical Account of Argyleshire* (1843) it says that the Clan Donald always kept the fortifications at Dunaverty 'in good repair and well guarded, as only from this position could the communications with Antrim be kept open and safe'.

There is no doubt that in past ages Dunaverty Castle must have appeared impregnable both from land and sea, a sullen place, offering no point of weakness to an invader. But today, when closely examined, its sparse, overgrown ruins reveal in places the effects of fire and violent assault. This is not surprising, because its whole history was a violent one, providing evidence that in the face of determined enemies no physical bastion is impregnable.

News of the castle goes back as far as the twelfth century. It was held by Somerled's descendant Angus Mor (Big Angus), the eldest son of Donald, from whom all the MacDonalds derive their surname. He lost it for a time to King Alexander III of Scotland, who was jealous of the growing power of the Lords of the Isles and came marching into Kintyre to demonstrate his authority. He, in turn, lost it to King Haco of Norway in 1263. Afterwards King Haco, who seems to have been a much more reasonable and statesman-like 'viking' than many biased chroniclers have made out, restored it to the MacDonalds.

Angus Mor's son, Angus Og (Young Angus), was a stout supporter of Robert the Bruce. After the disastrous Battle of Methven, Bruce fled to Kintyre, where Angus Og willingly provided refuge. The distinguished fugitive was first concealed at Saddell Castle on the east coast of the peninsula, then in the more secure fortress of Dunaverty; and when even Dunaverty became unsafe, he was taken secretly across the narrow sea to Rathlin. There, in another MacDonald Castle whose ruins today distinctly resemble those at Dunaverty, he was at last able to rest secure from his enemies. And have his notable confrontation with a spider.

Though Angus Og was a king's man, in later years the Clan Donald again became disillusioned with 'authority'.

In 1494 James IV brought an imposing army to Kintyre and seized Dunaverty, placing in it a garrison amply provided with artillery and gunners. At that time the representative of the MacDonalds in Kintyre was Sir John Cahanagh, a MacDonald by blood but so named from having been fostered in Antrim with the O'Cahans. Sir John, enraged by the King's actions, secretly assembled an army of his own – in Islay, Kintyre and Antrim – and awaited an opportunity to expel the royal garrison. The Rev. George Hill, in *The MacDonells of Antrim*, now takes up the story: 'The King, not anticipating any opposition to his arrangements, was in the act of sailing away with his personal attendants from the Mull [of Kintyre], when Sir John stormed Dunaverty, and actually hung the governor from the wall, in sight of the King and his departing ships.'

King James was unable to avenge the insult at the time; but years later, through the treachery of a jealous kinsman, Sir John and two of his sons were seized at Finlagan Castle in Islay and taken as the King's prisoners to Edinburgh. There they were found guilty of high treason and 'executed on the Burrowmuir, their bodies being buried in the church of St Anthony'.

From that time the MacDonalds were continually at variance with what today might be called 'the establishment'. Growing numbers of the clan crossed the narrow sea from Kintyre to Antrim, hoping to find there a more peaceable existence. But, being supporters of Mary Queen of Scots, they were natural enemies of Elizabeth of England, and, in consequence, Elizabeth's Irish Deputy, the Earl of Sussex, made sure that peace remained a word unknown to them.

Nor were the activities of Sussex confined to Ireland. He himself submitted to his sovereign the report of a punitive expedition he carried out in September 1558. On the 19th, in the ship *Mary Willoughby*, he 'arrived at Lowghe Cylkerran [Kinloch Kilchiaran, now Campbeltown] in Kintyre. On the same day I landed and burned eight miles of length, and therwith James McConell's [MacDonald's] chief house callit Saudell [Saddell] a fayre pile and a stronge. The neixte day, I crossed over the lande, and burned twelve myles of length on the other side of the Lowghe, wherein were burned a faire house callit Mawher Imore [Machrimore in Southend], and a strong castell callit Dunalvere [Dunaverty].'

(Sussex was a poor speller but obviously a man of action and an exemplar for all future Empire-builders.)

By 1647, however, the MacDonalds were back in Dunaverty; but now, when Cromwell was the 'authority', they had become King's men again. Their ancient rivals, the Campbells, had taken up arms on the other side; and when General David Leslie was ordered to subdue the rebel MacDonalds in the west, the Marquis of Argyle eagerly accepted an invitation to accompany him and to add a large quota of Campbell clansmen to an already considerable army. Boldly they marched through Dumbarton to Argyll and down upon Kintyre.

Sir Alexander MacDonald made an effort to stop them at a place called Rhunahaorine, a few miles south of Tarbert; but his cavalry floundered to disaster in a peat-bog (which is still there) and he and most of his army were forced to retreat 'in small shippes' to Islay. 'Here,' as is recorded in the *Account of the Clan MacLean*, 'the brave MacDonald made his last stand against the enemies of the King, but finding his position in too precarious a state to hope for success by opposition, or for mercy by submission, he immediately passed over to Ireland.'

A small force of 300 men, however, 'consisting mainly of MacDougalls and soldiers from Antrim', was left behind to defend Dunaverty. This was under the command of Archibald Og MacDonald of Sanda, a direct descendant of Sir John Cahanagh, 'traitorously put to death by James IV'.

For six weeks Leslie and Argyle besieged the castle; but in a hot, rainless June the water in the only well ran dry (occasionally it still runs dry in summer), and in the end it was thirst that defeated the garrison. Archibald Og MacDonald and his men surrendered to 'the mercy of the kingdom', and the mercy of the kingdom, as might have been expected, was death. 'Every mother's son,' wrote Sir John Turner, Leslie's adjutant, 'was put to the sword, except one young man, MacCoul [Mac-Dougall], whose life I begged, to be sent to France, with one hundred country fellows, whom we had smoked out of a cave, as they do foxes.'

An account of the massacre given in the *Memoirs of Montrose* (Vol. II) brings a chill to the heart: 'Having surrendered their arms, the Marquis of Argyle and a bloody preacher, Mr John Nevoy [minister of Loudon parish in Ayrshire and chaplain to Leslie's army] prevailed with him [Leslie] to break his word; and so the army was let loose upon them, and killed them all without mercy; whereat David Leslie seemed to have some inward check: For, while the Marquis and he, Mr Nevoy, were walking over their ankles in blood, he turned about and said, – "Now, Mass John, have you not, for once, gotten your fill of blood?" This was reported by many who heard it.'

Before leaving Southend, Leslie and Argyle set fire to the empty fortress, and afterwards the Castle was allowed to crumble into decay. Two centuries later the bones of the dead were gathered by descendants of the Clan Donald and buried in a common grave. A bleak, rectangular monument, it stands on the bare shoulder of an arable field near the Rock. The field is known to us as *machair a caistel*, 'the field of the castle'.

The massacre of Dunaverty is still spoken of in Southend as if it had happened yesterday.

There is a peat-fire legend about the wife of a Clan Donald soldier to whom the Campbells offered amnesty if, with her baby on her back, she could climb the sheer cliff on the east side of the rock. She climbed it. But as her clutching hands appeared on the summit a young Campbell officer slashed them off with his sword and she and her baby fell ninety feet to their deaths. That day the cliff was given a Gaelic name: 'The Cliff of the Falling Woman'.

Next morning, with the Castle burning, Leslie's army began to march away. As the Campbells, in the rear, were passing through the village of Southend (then called Muneroy), the young officer's horse reared and bolted. He was thrown from the saddle, but his foot caught in a stirrup and he was dragged screaming for help along the rough road beyond the village. His men and the villagers who watched – all of them aware of his action on the previous day – gave no sign that they saw or heard. The horse ran free, swerving from side to side, dashing its rider to pieces against the boulders by the roadside.

Another memory is of the plague brought to Southend by Leslie's army. It is said that hundreds of local people died and that at one time, in the autumn of 1647, 'only two chimneys were left smoking' in the parish.

As boys in the Manse, my brothers and I were eager listeners to the savage tales about Dunaverty, some told by the Padre, some by old men and women whose families had been involved. We appreciated their drama and romance and were scarcely aware of the cruelty, greed and utter contempt for human life and dignity which lay behind them. Vaguely we apprehended that St Columba, the disciple of love, would not have approved of them; but it seemed to us, at the time, that during the past few hundred years standards of behaviour in Britain had changed for the better and that such bloody events could now occur only among ignorant foreign tribes. Contemporary writers of boys' fiction encouraged us in this belief. The slaughter of Red Indians, Zulus and other 'lesser breeds without the law' left us proud and reassured, confident in our British rectitude. It was a traumatic experience when we began to realize that the massacre of millions in two great 'white' wars, with the unending political and sectarian massacres in Ireland on the side, demonstrated that our so-called 'western civilization' could produce an even lower level of conduct than that which had once been ascribed to fictional 'wogs'.

But though this particular sealed loft, when we opened it, offered appalling discoveries, it gave us comfort, too, in a story of human kindness which shone clear among the drab and wicked debris of Dunaverty. I have already told it in *Salt in My Porridge*; but I think it bears repeating – as the Padre kept on doing in his sermons – if only because it provides evidence that the bad in human nature is generally balanced by the good.

The wife of Archibald Og MacDonald, the commander of the Dunaverty garrison, had died in the early part of 1647, leaving him with a baby son, James Ranald. James Ranald was with his father in the Castle when the siege began, looked after by an eighteen-year-old Southend girl called Flora Mac-Cambridge.

On the night before the massacre, putting no trust in 'the mercy of the kingdom', Flora made a plan to save the baby. Round him she wrapped a plaid of Campbell tartan which had belonged to a prisoner captured during the siege. Then, carrying him in her arms, she crept down from the Rock and, in the moonlight, began to run across the beach, away from Dunaverty, away from threatening death. But soon, while still stumbling barefoot over the wet, ribbed sand, she was stopped by a Campbell sentry. Her heart thumped in her throat.

'I am the wife of a Campbell soldier,' she said. 'See, my son wears the tartan.'

The sentry lifted a corner of the plaid. 'Strange!' he said. 'A Campbell mother whose baby has the MacDonald eyes! But go your way, girl. I have no quarrel with women or children.'

So Flora went to a cave under the cliff at Keil, and there, feeding him on sheeps' tallow and ewes' milk, she hid and attended to James Ranald until Leslie and Argyle had gone.

James Ranald grew up and eventually, by patient negotiation, brought about a lasting peace between the MacDonalds and the Campbells. He lies buried in the graveyard of Keil-colm-cille, just over the wall from the big cave in which he and Flora found refuge.

The population of Southend has often been described as one-third Lowland, one-third Highland and one-third Irish. The Rev. Kenneth MacLeod of Gigha – the author of 'The Road to the Isles' – used to say that the Padre was one-third Protestant, one-third Roman Catholic and one-third pagan, an opinion with which my mother agreed. Was this a clue to the success of his long ministry in the parish?

There is no doubt that like everybody else in Southend he had a 'soft side' for the Irish and a continuing interest in the history of the 'connection'. History is people, he used to say, and people are still making it.

Our accents and our dialect owe much to Ireland. Perhaps the best example of how we used to talk (how we still talk when the mood comes on us) is found in a 'Come-all-ye' in praise of a girl called 'Flory Loynachan'. (The surname Loynachan has become Lang in more modern times, and Flora Langs are common in Kintyre today.) The 'poem' was written in the early part of last century by a Kintyrean of Irish stock called O'Brol-lochan, who, while studying at Glasgow University to become a minister of the Free Church, changed his name to Brodie. The tune comes from Ireland.

I heard the song for the first time from Willie McKerral, Jean's father, who kept chuckling as my face registered frequent incomprehension. It is often sung at local ceilidhs, when the whisky flows. Here is part of it:

> O, it buitie be an ogly thing
> That mougres thus ower me,
> For I scrabbed at masel yestreen
> An' couldna bab an e'e.
> My he'rt is a' tae muilins minched,
> Brye, smuirach, daps an' gum.
> I'm a poor cruichach spalyin' scrae,
> My horts ha'e struck me dumb.

> Dear Flory Loynachan, if thou
> Through Saana Soun' were tossed,
> An' rouchled like a shoggie-shoo
> In a veshal wi' wan mast;
> Though the nicht were makin' for a roil,
> Though ralliach were the sea,
> Though scorlins warpled my thowl pins,
> My shallop wad reach thee.

> Were I the laird o' Achnaglach,
> Or Kilmanshenachan fair,
> Cnockstaplemore, Kilwheepnach,
> Feochaig or Ballochgair;
> Did I inherit Tayinraich,
> Drumgarve or Ballochantuy,
> Christlach or Kerran – daing the bit,
> I'd fauchit them a' for thee.

A rough 'translation' of the first two verses:

'O, it must be a terrible affliction that has come over me, because last night I kept scratching myself and couldn't close an eye. My heart is all minced up like meal, like dross or other types of coal debris. I'm a poor creature, staggering about. My hurts, my wounds, have struck me dumb.

'Dear Flory Loynachan, if you were being tossed about in Sanda Sound, shaken as if you were on a swing, in a vessel with only one mast: though the night threatened a storm and the sea was exceedingly rough, though seaweed wrapped itself round my rowlocks, my small boat would reach you.'

The last verse lists a number of farms still in existence and still with the same names in South Kintyre. Even though he became the owner of all these places the anguished lover declares that – damn the opposition – he would give them all away in exchange for Flory.

As they say, 'Whaur's yer Anglo-Saxon noo?'

Our parents, both native Gaelic speakers, found no difficulty in understanding the 'Come-all-ye's'. Many of the apparently outlandish words are derived from the Irish Gaelic. Others, of Lowland origin, were in everyday use in Southend during the whole of my father's ministry, from 1910 to 1957.

When Flory Loynachan was top of the pops in Southend, 150 years ago, cross-channel boats plied regularly between Cushendun, in Red Bay, and Dunaverty. Each had an individual name but, in general, was known locally as the Black Wherry. Passengers were often debtors or petty thieves trying to escape justice; cargoes sometimes contained contraband – salt, soap, hides, horses, wool – and excisemen in Kintyre and Antrim had a busy time of it, keeping an eye on the people and the goods it carried. Burke was one of the criminals who sailed in the Black Wherry and was able to avoid arrest.

A short, thick-set man with round shoulders, at the time in his middle thirties, Burke was the son of a farmer in County Tyrone, who had been, in turn, baker, cobbler, weaver and militiaman. After a quarrel with his family he deserted the militia and crossed the narrow sea to Scotland. Most writers on criminology accept the supposition that he met Hare in Edinburgh in 1826.

About Hare's origins little seems to be known, but a contemporary pamphleteer described him as a long, thin man, physically Burke's opposite. With their prostitute companions, Helen MacDougall and Maggie Laird, the two men 'shacked up' together in Log's Boarding House in Tanner's Close. There –

and later at a house in Gibbs Close – they carried on a trade as 'body-snatchers', opening graves and selling corpses to doctors and medical students. Their most regular customer was Dr Knox of 10 Surgeon's Square, who sometimes paid as much as £7 10s for a fresh cadaver. When they were unable to unearth a suitable body they resorted to murder, picking their victims from the beggars, cinder women, harlots and other flotsam of the Edinburgh streets.

> Burke's the murderer, Hare's the thief,
> And Knox the boy who buys the beef.

Justice eventually overtook the vicious pair when a beggar couple named Grey, who had been lodging with them at Gibbs Close, found the blood-stained corpse of another beggar woman in Burke's room and informed the police. At the trial in the High Court of Justiciary in Edinburgh, Hare turned King's evidence and, in consequence, was not tried. Neither was Maggie Laird. The case against Helen MacDougall resulted in a 'not proven' verdict; but Burke was found guilty and sentenced to death. Dr Knox was not even asked to give evidence.

During his time in the condemned cell Burke complained continually that Dr Knox had swindled him over payment for some of the bodies. This obsession with money also caused him to demand a fee of sixpence from curious visitors who wanted to sketch him. He was hanged on 28 January 1829.

What happened to Hare is a mystery. There is a story that he went to the Midlands of England to work in a lime-kiln and that when his identity was discovered his workmates blinded him with quicklime. But could this be a Victorian 'morality'? What seems certain is that he died as a blind old beggar in London.

Our Southend legend, which we learnt as boys with ghoulish delight, insists that Burke and Hare came from Ireland together, in the Black Wherry. They stayed the night at the local inn – the Argyll Arms – and in a drunken brawl killed a man whose body they concealed under the ice in the Carr Loch (where we used to find the tadpoles and where our whiskery elders enjoyed winter curling). I once wrote a short story based on this piece of apocrypha. The story itself was bad, but I still think the title I gave it was inspirational: *Frozen Stiff*.

The brave tales of olden times in Southend are matched by more modern ones. Any visitors who come to enjoy a holiday in our 'sleepy little parish' are always surprised to discover just how much goes on. We attract spies, fugitives and unusual characters, the like of which James Bond, in his tiny metropolitan world of blondes and fast cars, never dreamed of.

Our spy scares have been numerous, not without reason. The Mull of Kintyre overlooks the North Channel, the main convoy route out of Britain. In the two wars, any stranger appearing among us with a sketching-block was bound to come under suspicion.

In the first summer of the Second World War, while recuperating after a long illness and awaiting 'call up', I captured a spy myself.

I had enrolled as a special constable, with instructions to maintain close liaison with the Local Defence Volunteers. (Later the LDV became the Home Guard.) One afternoon a friend of mine, an LDV corporal, rang me up with the news that an individual carrying an easel and paints had been spotted on the moors above the Mull of Kintyre. He was now on his way down to the village of Southend. If I got cracking I could intercept him on the road near Keil.

I met him just beyond the graveyard, under the high cliffs. He was broad-faced, clean-shaven, loose-limbed and tall, with blond streaks in his thick, untidy hair. He wore spectacles, heavy brogues and stockings, a khaki shirt and what I imagined was a German-looking pair of short 'shorts'. We exchanged wary words, and though he spoke good English I was immediately suspicious of what sounded to me like a heavy guttural accent. I asked for proofs of his identity. His papers appeared to be in order, but when I looked inside his knapsack and saw the sketches and paintings he had made I came to a decision.

The Campbeltown police had been visiting the island of Sanda that day, examining the body of a sailor found on the shore. They were expected back in the late afternoon; and, indeed, just as I finished interrogating my suspect, their boat swung round the Bow Reef and entered the bay, heading for Dunaverty.

I took my man and handed him over to them. They whisked him away in their car, and, as far as I was concerned, that appeared to be the end of it. The following month I was called up.

Four years later, at Anzio, when at last the Allies had broken out, I was asked to help in arranging a piping programme by the bands of all the Scottish regiments in the area. An officer from the Gordon Highlanders came to see me about it. Into my dug-out descended the tall, loose-limbed figure of Captain Hamish Henderson, wearing German-looking shorts and greeting me in a Caithness accent as thick as mine from Kintyre. We recognized each other at once. He was my 'spy'.

With his poetic genius, his quick humour and love for all the Scottish arts, Hamish has remained my friend. He tells me that my story is a load of rubbish, full of inaccuracies, and that the Campbeltown police never suspected him for a single minute. Maybe not. But, as we both found during our stints as temporary soldiers, life can be complicated for a writer whose capital is his imagination, especially during a war.

But it seems that while Hamish Henderson and I were disporting ourselves in foreign parts, a real German spy did make a brief appearance in Southend. When I became a civilian again I heard part of the story from my neighbour, Archie Cameron the salmon-fisher, who actually met the spy making his way towards the jetty at Dunaverty.

'He was a good-looking young fellow, about six feet tall, with blue eyes and a fresh complexion,' Archie told me. 'He carried a knapsack and wore RAF uniform. I thought he was an airman home on leave. I came across him at the golf-course gate and said hullo, and he mumbled something in reply. I was hurrying to the Post Office at the time, to phone the police in Campbeltown about a tug that had gone aground on Sanda, and I thought no more about him.

'When I returned from the Post Office I noticed that Dick Gillon's old sailing boat was missing from the jetty, along with a pair of oars from one of my own small boats. I looked out to sea, and sure enough there the boat was, heading south towards the Irish Sea. I thought nothing about that, either. I was sure it was Dick, that he had taken a notion to go fishing.

'A few minutes later I got the shock of my life. I saw Dick walking across the shore, approaching the jetty. I remembered the young fellow then all right and alerted the Coastguards, who at once got in touch with the authorities.

'By this time Dick's stolen boat was out of sight and Dick himself was hopping mad. Southend was in an uproar. I kept wondering if I would get into trouble for leaving the oars unguarded in my small boat, because it was a regulation during war-time that oars must be locked away when not in use.'

Much to his relief, nobody since then has ever mentioned oars to Archie. In the meantime, however, high-powered action was taking place in other quarters. This is described in dramatic detail by Captain Jack Broome in his book, *Convoy is to Scatter*.

Captain Broome was in command of Escort Group One, in the destroyer *Keppel*. He had been summoned to Greenock to attend a conference on a troop convoy which his Group was to pick up off Northern Ireland the following morning. This convoy, one of the largest and most important of the Second World War, was due to sail around the Cape, carrying the basic elements of what was to be the Eighth Army.

'When the conference was over,' Captain Broome writes, 'I looked at my watch and found that instead of staying overnight and sailing with the convoy, I had plenty of time to get down the Clyde, into Loch Foyle and up the river to Londonderry, for all to enjoy a final night ashore with wives, families or girl friends, before sailing early to pick up our convoy.'

The *Keppel* cleared the Cumbraes. Her speed increased until she was thundering along at thirty-two knots. The officers chatted on the bridge. Suddenly the radio officer buzzed through to say that a top-priority cypher from the Admiralty had just been received and was being decoded.

In a few minutes Captain Broome was reading the signal aloud: 'ENEMY AGENT KNOWN TO HAVE BEEN IN ALDERSHOT RECENTLY SEEN YESTERDAY IN GREENOCK MINGLING WITH TROOPS EMBARKING OVERSEAS CONVOY. MOTOR BOAT BELONGING LIGHT-HOUSE-KEEPER MULL OF KINTYRE REPORTED MISSING 0900 TODAY WEDNESDAY. CONSIDER POSSIBLE AGENT HAS STOLEN BOAT AND NOW MAKING FOR IRISH FREE STATE WITH IMPORTANT INFORMA-TION ABOUT CONVOY SAILING TOMORROW. MOTOR SKIFF HULL GREEN RUBBING STRAKE ORANGE. TANK FULL. MAN 6 FEET FAIR FRESH COMPLEXION LAST SEEN WEARING KHAKI BATTLE DRESS. NO OTHER SHIP OR ANY AIRCRAFT AVAILABLE. SEARCH FOR BOAT. REPORT WHEN YOU HAVE FOUND IT.'

I have no idea how the Admiralty got the impression that the spy was wearing battle-dress, that it was a lighthouse-keeper's boat he had stolen or that the boat in question was coloured green and orange and had a motor. In fact, according to Archie Cameron – and also to my friend Duncan Watson, then an auxiliary coastguard – he was wearing RAF uniform and the boat was an old scow, encrusted with black tar, whose only motive power consisted of oars and a home-made sail.

Captain Broome, the first lieutenant and the navigator studied the chart. After a calculation involving the estimated speed of the stolen boat and the strength of the wind and tides, they decided to follow a course almost due south. They had only forty-five minutes of daylight left to find their man. If they failed, and the spy was able to contact the German Embassy in Dublin, Captain Broome dared not think of what might happen to the convoy.

By this time the *Keppel*'s crew were on deck, eager volunteer look-outs. Captain Broome offered a free pint to the first man who spotted the boat.

In the next few minutes a number of false alarms were raised, and when finally the mast-head look-out reported an object in the water some five miles ahead, Captain Broome was guarded in his enthusiasm. If the boat possessed a motor it ought to have been much further south. But then, looking through his telescope, the chief yeoman sang out in some excitement: 'There is something there, be Jesus!'

Course was altered slightly to the bearing given, and as the destroyer closed a message from the chief yeoman came down the mast-head blow-pipe: 'It's a boat, one bloke in it, 'e's trying to row it, an' I reckon it's my pint.'

The *Keppel* got close enough for her crew to see that the boat was stopped and that the man, leaning over a heavy pair of oars, looked exhausted. 'My job is looking after fishermen, and there's a storm coming up,' Captain Broome shouted down through a loud-hailer. 'If you're in difficulties I'll hoist you inboard and take you to the Irish coast.'

The spy raised an assenting arm.

As an escort led him up to the bridge, the first thing Captain Broome noticed were his hands clutching the ladder rail. They were oily and raw.

'I've been rowing for two hours,' he explained in excellent English. 'Trying to get back.'

'Back where?'

'I'm on leave. I borrowed the boat from a friend and promised to return it before dark.'

At that moment the first lieutenant, who had been instructed to search the boat and everything in it, arrived on the bridge. Standing behind the man he held up a small book. Almost incredibly, it was *Mein Kampf*, in German.

The man looked over his shoulder and saw the book. With a shrug and a wry smile he turned back to the Captain and said: 'All right, you win.'

By this time it was almost dark. A message was sent: 'ADMIRALTY FROM KEPPEL. MOST IMMEDIATE. YOUR BOAT RECOVERED. MAN ARRESTED.'

The spy was taken to Larne and handed over to the Army. The *Keppel* resumed its passage to Londonderry, only two hours late. Next morning the convoy sailed. It never lost a ship.

Much to his indignation, Dick Gillon didn't get his boat back. Somebody in Larne, he often complained to me, must have 'nicked it'. However, months later, the new 'owner' seems to have had a pang of conscience, because Dick received an envelope through the post which contained a pound note and a written message: 'For the boat.'

Dick lived in Southend until he was ninety-two, telling the tale of the spy who stole his boat. I'm glad he never knew the contents of the Admiralty's message to *Keppel*. Like most of us, Dick was averse to sharing the limelight – especially, in his case, with an undeserving lighthouse-keeper.

Another, less obvious example of an Irish 'connection' occurred in South Kintyre more than ten years ago when Paul McCartney of the Beatles bought the small farm of High Park, a few miles north of Campbeltown. He received warm greetings from us all. One reason is that Kintyre is full of McCartneys whose ancestors crossed the North Channel from Ireland just as Paul's did on their way to Liverpool. Another reason was that St Columba left us with some good advice, which we have never forgotten: 'Always be hospitable to a stranger.'

We hoped that Paul and Jane Asher, who was his constant companion at the beginning, would not remain strangers for long. We liked the look of them both.

For a time Paul and Jane (and many of their friends) were our intermittent neighbours, welcome at local dances and cattle-sales. Even Old Sandy, a notorious 'wit', got tired of repeating his dead-pan joke: 'I tell ye, the prophecy has come true – when the moles reach the Mull of Kintyre the beetles will follow! God help my potatoes!'

Unhappily, through the years, Paul's visits to High Park have become fewer and fewer, though he and his American wife do sometimes stay there for a night or two. His conviction at Campbeltown Sheriff Court on a drugs charge has also tended to mar the picture. Perhaps Paul – like us – has been searching for a human ideal which just doesn't exist.

3

Chauffeur to a Rabbit

With its stories, its wide fresh spaces and kindly people, Southend was always full of metaphoric light as far as we in the Manse were concerned. Electric light, however, did not come to the parish until 1950.

During the Second World War, while campaigning in Italy, I was astonished to discover that all the villages we occupied – even those perched precariously on mountain tops – were efficiently linked to the public electricity supply. At home my wife and parents still struggled along with paraffin lamps and coal-fired stoves. (Some stoves in Southend, of a superior variety, were at this period fuelled by anthracite. Jean wrote to tell me how Barbara, her daily help, had arrived one morning full of enthusiasm for a friend's new 'anti-Christ' cooker.)

Once, in a village near Potenza in Southern Italy, where the 2nd Royal Scots Fusiliers happened to be 'resting', one of my sergeants, Jack Hibbett from Oakham, had a kindly inspiration to do something about my birthday. Having heard me talk of a Scottish 'clootie dumpling', he decided to make one and cook it on an electric stove 'liberated' from the local village hall. It turned out to be a beauty.

As I tucked into it that night, ravenous after a day's 'recce' in the hills, I complimented him. 'Superb! Just the right degree of toughness in the skin and of melting consistency inside. How on earth did you manage it?'

'Well, sir, I did exactly what it said in that *People's Journal* you showed me. I got most of the ingredients from the cook – flour, baking soda, sugar, suet, treacle, tinned milk watered down. In the grocer's shop along the street I managed to find some raisins and spices. I mixed the whole shooting-match in a bowl, brought a big pot of water to the boil on the electric stove and popped the dumpling in.'

'After wrapping it in a "cloot" – or cloth, as you Sassenachs would call it?'

'That's right, sir. Though actually the cloth I used was one of your vests – or semmits, as you Scots call them. There was nothing else handy.'

I still say it was one of the best 'clootie dumplings' I have ever tasted.

With the crossing from Ireland during the first few centuries AD of a tribe known as the *Scotti* – amongst whose number was St Columba – Southend experienced Christian civilization long before most other places in Scotland. Apparently, however, the ruling classes considered that moral and spiritual benefits were enough for us to be going on with. Material benefits were always tardy in reaching our 'neck of the woods'.

Old Mrs MacSporran of the plump cheeks, black-bodiced bosom and ample skirts, who lived in Keil Lodge, a quarter of a mile along the road from Achnamara, used to tell us that when she was a child her parents had lit their cottage with a 'croosie' (from the Gaelic *cruiskan*, a small dish of oil with a wick in it) and that she herself, as a housewife, had used in succession candles, plain paraffin lamps, pressure lamps (such as the Aladdin) and finally, when she was approaching ninety, 'the electrics'.

Housing conditions in Southend were also poor until the decade before the Second World War, when the Padre, along with other sympathetic county councillors, translated into action the idea of subsidized houses for farm-workers. It must be admitted that thatched roofs had almost completely disappeared; but baths and indoor toilets were available only in the 'big hooses' like Macharioch, where the Dowager Duchess lived, and Carskiey, built in the early years of the century by Mrs Boyd, a member of the Coats family, whose thread-mills had brought new work to Paisley. The occupiers of less privileged dwellings had to use, for bathing, zinc tubs filled with hot water and, for toilet purposes, either outside earthen closets or handy hedges. Windows were small and ceilings low; even in the farms chimneys smoked. Damp invaded rooms not constantly fired.

And yet, in those years before, during and immediately after the First World War, the food we ate in Southend – in respect of taste at any rate – was far superior to the processed, pre-packaged, carefully analysed diet we are offered today. Aeration and pasteurization, cans, cartons and deep freezes were all unknown. As a result, most of what appeared on our plates was natural and fresh.

Milk, straight from the cow, tasted like milk. Potatoes, unforced by artificial manures, were ambrosial compared with the watery blobs, encased in plastic, which come from the supermarkets. Bread had hard, crunchy crusts. Slices of a thickness relevant to our hunger could be cut from a loaf which smelt not of a factory but of a real bake-house. Nowadays a loaf is as neutral as cotton wool and turns green and sour if a housewife looks the other way. As far as I am concerned, the invention of sliced bread was a disaster.

I watch my neighbours' children, on a cold winter's day, daintily eating wafer-thin potato-crisps and washing them down with chilly 'coke'. What do they know of the sustaining 'jeely pieces', accompanied by a glass of milk, which always rewarded us after a day at school? (The 'jeely piece' or 'chuck' as we used to call it, consisted of a thickly cut, thickly buttered slice of bread folded over to enclose a dripping layer of, more often than not, home-made bramble jelly.)

As a family in the Manse, though poor financially, we fed like princes. The Padre's parishioners were generous. Few of them paid a social call without bearing gifts.

Potatoes. Field turnips. Pats of churn-made butter, stamped with the design traditionally favoured by the farm it came from. 'Trotters' for roasting when a pig was killed. A 'sheep's heid' from which the blacksmith would remove wool and hair by singeing so that it could be used for sumptuous broth. Healthy outdoor chickens which would boil or roast deliciously instead of turning into the tasteless bits of slimy rubber which result from the cooking of birds reared in batteries (or deep litters) and then frozen. All these, from time to time, were given us by the farmers, whose kindness was remarkable considering the poor state of agriculture at the time.

From the 'big hooses' and from the 'toffs' who crowded the Argyll Arms Hotel during the shooting season there came pheasants, grouse and woodcock, which Maimie would hang in the scullery for the requisite number of days and then pluck thoroughly, meanwhile cursing in the Gaelic at the intricacy and tediousness of the operation. The fishing tenants presented us with salmon and sea-trout clean run from the Atlantic.

(It may be mentioned here that the Padre's family, in an emergency, could also provide the occasional pheasant or salmon captured by unconventional means.)

Less exotic but no less delicious gifts of food were often left on the Manse doorstep by anonymous benefactors. These included rabbits, wood pigeons and hares. Such benefactors were always known to us, but as moral and legal complications might have arisen had the offerings been made in person, their deeds were always crowned by a halo – admittedly slightly crooked – of anonymous righteousness.

Rabbit stew, with turnips, carrots, onions and thick gravy, was a meal greatly favoured by us boys. In later years, when an increasing rabbit population threatened the corn fields, and anxious farmers introduced myxomatosis, nobody wanted to eat rabbit any more and another nourishing and tasty dish disappeared from local menus.

Recently, however, in Southend at any rate, a lusty breed of rabbit has evolved which shows signs of being immune from the disease. Sporting types from the village are often to be seen in the high fields and on the golf course, armed with ferrets, nets, guns and eager whippets. The farmers raise no objection

to their hunting forays, because in a farmer's language rabbit is
a distasteful word. Rabbit stew is enjoyed again by some; but
Jean, implacably, refuses to let me join their number.

When myxomatosis was at its height in the parish, the roads
near Achnamara crawled with blind rabbits, festering and
slowly dying. They seemed to move close to human beings as if
pleading for help, though no help, apart from a quick death to
relieve their misery, was possible. Jean can never forget, and I
don't blame her. Like Jock, our son, her attitude to all animals
is affectionate and personal.

For example . . .

Last summer a young rabbit entered and took up residence
in Achnamara garden. During the night watches, while I slept,
it began to feed with enthusiasm on my lettuce and cabbage
plants. I vowed vengeance.

. Its hiding place was under a disorganized clump of heath and
veronica, and it became expert at dodging my mad beatings
with a spade or graip around the periphery of the bushes.
Sometimes I glimpsed it far down, lurking in a tangle of twigs
and leaves. I would make a quick thrust, but long before the
spade or graip reached the target area it would move slinkily
and silently to a safer spot. No matter how hard I tried I was
unable to chase it out into the open, where the advantage would
be mine. I had a feeling it was laughing at me.

Jean became schizophrenic. On the one hand she sympathized
with me for having worked so hard in the garden only to find my
succulent rewards being snatched away by a pirate. On the
other hand she was terrified that in my rage I would kill the
rabbit, which, using an epithet that didn't occur to me, she
described as a 'darling'. When I made my attacks on the bushes
she was always there, torn with anxiety concerning the outcome.

One morning I banged about with a graip and, no doubt in a
moment of drowsy unpreparedness caused by a night's gluttony
among the lettuces, the rabbit emerged. Only half grown, it
looked clean and fresh and smug. I made a wild lunge in its
direction but unfortunately tripped on a root of veronica and

fell among the cabbages. The rabbit hopped away with contemptuous ease and took cover behind a long concrete edging tile which lay against the wall of the garage.

But that was its error. I had it now. Brushing myself down, I approached the garage and held the graip high. 'Ease that tile away from the wall,' I instructed Jean.

'No, no, please! Don't kill him!'

'Don't kill him? That rabbit is a menace! Starving us to death!'

'Poor wee thing! He's lying in there, terrified!'

'I should hope so! Ease away the tile!'

'No, no, please. You realize what you're doing, don't you? You're playing God.'

'What?'

'You're always writing about St Columba. Remember that story you often tell about when he was a little boy and he bent down to take a trout from the river and the poet Gemman said to him "How would *you* like it if God stretched down His hand and tried to kill *you*?" '

'Give me strength!' I said.

'The poor wee rabbit hasn't much strength.'

'What has that got to do with it?'

'Everything,' she said.

I lowered the graip. 'Well, if I spare its blasted life it's not going to spend the remainder of it in my garden!'

'Of course not. Wait a minute.'

She put a hand under the tile and presently withdrew it holding the rabbit. Having fondled it, uttering low-pitched words of endearment, she said to me: 'Now, take out the car. Drive me down to the graveyard and I'll pop him over the wall. He'll find the best grass in the parish there.'

It was the first time I had played chauffeur to a rabbit, and I prayed that on our journey nobody would see us. Thankfully nobody did. The pirate was left to enjoy luxury among the tombstones, a fate much better than he deserved, and for the rest of the season the garden flourished.

Except for an assault by white maggots on my onion crop.

Nature, I have learned, is relentless, infinitely resourceful in its method of attack.

No rabbits on today's menus. Nor any pigeon pie. But there was a time when Donald MacLean, the gamekeeper, made sure that we feasted regularly on both.

Donald and his wife and young family lived in a cottage by the riverside, not far from the Manse. His son Neil was one of my school buddies. From Neil, who was slightly older, I learned a lot about the birds and the bees, in more senses than one. Many a painful confrontation we had with our respective parents when we arrived home, after scrambling about on a spring afternoon among the hedges, our knees and our jerseys and our wide patched short trousers looking as if a set of harrows had been dragged over them.

From Neil I learned also the finer arts of playing 'rounders', which used to be a popular game among boys in Scottish rural schools. He taught me how to make a good 'bat' by cutting a three-foot length from an old broom handle. He taught me, too, how to wield it with a well-timed flick of the wrist. He himself, a *coiteach* (or left-hander), was the longest hitter in the school – Southend's Babe Ruth – and when he picked me for his team I basked in the reflected glory.

Has it been proved that American baseball originated in 'rounders'? It is almost exactly similar, except that in our version there was no 'pitcher' and the batsman threw up the ball himself and then hit it a 'scud'. And we called the bases 'dales'. But, as in modern baseball, our clothes and our bodies were frequently damaged when, if in danger of being run out, we threw ourselves at the 'dales'.

Neil's father, Donald MacLean, a thin, wiry man, beardless but with a ponderous moustache, resembled my own in character, being in turn kind, authoritarian, compassionate and brittle-tempered. (In those days of large and hearty families a father, in order to maintain control, was almost bound to combine several contradictory roles.) As a by-product of his trade in dealing with wild-life, he was a keen pigeon fancier and kept a loft of racing birds. I don't know exactly what happens in the pigeon-racing world nowadays, but in Donald's time, fifty years ago, the arrangements for racing appear to have been, to say the least, perfunctory.

I'm still vague about when, how and where the birds were sent for 'take-off'. All I know is that on the day they were expected back at Donald's cottage, Neil, his sister and almost everybody at the Manse were conscripted to lend a hand. As far as Archie, Willie and I were concerned – and later, Rona, Kenneth and John – we were only too happy to take part. We owed Donald plenty, on account of his generosity with rabbits and wood pigeons; and, in any case, the sense of adventure and excitement engendered on a race day was much to our liking.

The method of timing the birds was peculiar. When one landed in the loft, a ring with an identifying number had to be taken from its leg and conveyed as quickly as possible to the nearest Justice of the Peace or minister of religion, who then entered on a form the bird's number, the exact time of the ring's delivery and, finally, his own signature. When a number of birds were involved, with the chance that some of them would arrive almost together, it can be imagined that problems of logistics were liable to intrude.

But Donald had an answer to those problems. It was man-power – or, to be more accurate, child-power.

From his cottage by the riverside a steep path, more than fifty yards in length, led up to a stile on the main road. From this stile to the Manse – where the Padre carried out double duty as a Justice of the Peace and minister of religion, the way was flat and less than half a mile. On a race day Donald would take up his position on the kennel roof, in which the pigeon loft was situated. Neil and his sisters would be stationed on the ground below. At the stile, high above, three of us would watch and wait, each with a bicycle. (One bicycle was mine, the one I had bought from Bobby Kelly; the others belonged to Donald and his family.)

When the first pigeon fluttered in Donald would whip the

ring off its leg and throw it down. Neil – for example – would catch it and go panting up the steep path to the stile, where he'd hand it over, say, to Willie. Willie would immediately leap on a bicycle and, crouching over the handlebars, pedal furiously down the road. At the Manse back gate, skidding to a stop, he would be met by Maimie and Rona (the latter now outgrowing the infant stage), who would go scuttling and screaming into the Manse, past my wide-eyed mother in the kitchen and along to the study. There the Padre would be esconced, probably composing a sermon – as a rule a race reached its climax on a Saturday afternoon – but also keeping a magisterial eye on the clock. The time would be registered, the form signed and the whole business would go into reverse.

In the meantime, if another bird returned to the loft – or even another two – more teams of relay runners and cyclists were ready to go into action. Indeed, I have known collisions to occur as one cyclist arrived breathless at the Manse back gate and another, equally breathless, was riding away again.

Donald had considerable success with his racing pigeons. But one day something happened which caused anguish not only in his eager heart but also in the hearts of us all.

The great champion of his loft – a cock pigeon of impeccable breeding – was entered for a valuable money prize, and Donald reckoned that if the bird were clocked in by three o'clock in the afternoon he would have a good chance of winning it. By two o'clock Donald was on the roof, waiting beside the loft. The relay teams were at their posts. All systems were 'go'. Eyes were focussed on a patch of blue sky above the plantation which flanked the cottage. If the champion flew true to form it was in this patch that he would first appear.

At about two forty-five he did appear, like a tiny, grey-white piece of thistledown floating in the sun. A cry went up from Donald, in his lisping, burring tongue: 'Here he comes! The wee beauty! The wee beauty!' The relay teams uttered wild cheers. Individuals, eager to gain the honour of carrying the ring, began jostling for position.

Closer came the champion, swinging down. Twenty feet above the loft he ceased to descend and began, instead, to fly in circles. 'Come, my wee pet!' cooed Donald. 'Come on, now! Come on!'

The champion ignored him. He flew round and round, displaying beautiful technique but making no effort to land. Cold currents of dismay drifted among us.

'Come doon!' demanded Donald, the voice so recently filled with love and pride now changing to one of sharp authority. 'D'ye hear me – come doon!'

There was no response. Watches were consulted. It was five minutes to three.

Donald, on the roof, was hopping from foot to foot, supplicating arms held high, rage held in difficult check. 'What's the matter, boy? This is me. Come on, come tae me!'

Still no response.

Finally, inevitably, Donald's temper cracked. 'Throw me up a gun!' he shouted to Neil, below.

Fearful, but not daring to disobey, his son did so. Donald shouldered the weapon and held the barrels high. 'Come doon, ye wee bugger!' he roared with passion. 'Come doon, ye wee bugger, or I'll shoot ye doon!'

He had no intention of doing anything of the sort, of course, except in imagination; but we all held our breaths. Neil's sisters covered their eyes with their hands and began to cry. The time was three o'clock.

The champion performed another coy circle. Then, with infinite grace, he flew slowly down and settled on the stock of Donald's gun.

The brown, lean, gamekeeper's face was parchment tight. He caught the bird, oxtered the gun, slipped off the ring and threw it down to Neil. Neil dashed up the steep path, handed it to Willie at the stile. Two minutes later Maimie and Rona were invading the quiet of the Padre's study.

But the time certified was seven minutes past three. It was anti-climax. It was failure. We all sensed it.

A week later, when the results came through, Donald's champion had lost the race by two minutes.

At the time nobody derived much pleasure from the affair, with the exception, perhaps, of the Padre, who declared it had sparked off an idea for a sermon. I don't think Donald was amused when he heard the text: 'And the dove came in to him in the evening; and, lo, in her mouth was an olive leaf pluckt off: so Noah knew that the waters were abated from off the earth.' No doubt he envied Noah's possession of an amenable pigeon and brooded darkly on the recalcitrance of his own 'wee bugger'.

What amazes me, looking back, is the simple innocence – and honesty – of it all.

Fifty years ago, the system of timing a pigeon race would appear to have been open to all kinds of 'rackets'. Donald could have sent the Padre phoney rings. The Padre, as a close friend, could have 'adjusted' the time certificates. On the day of the big race, for example, he might have decided that, in justice, he ought to disregard the fraught interval before the actual landing and clock in the champion at the time it arrived above the loft. But to my father – and to Donald – such ideas simply did not occur. Standards had been set. They found no reason to question them.

In this modern, 'sophisticated' age, are standards of any kind held in such straightforward regard? It would seem not, if notice be taken of the propaganda which delights in 'interpreting' standards for political, and – sometimes – religious purposes. No wonder we are hemmed in by so many self-propagating rules and regulations, so many Royal Commissions, civil servants, local government officials and accountants. Nobody trusts anybody else any more.

If my nature weren't basically optimistic I think I would despair at all the narking and nagging that goes on. Political parties snarl at one another, forgetting that their business is to do their best for the country, not for the little kingdoms of Toryism and Socialism. The CBI and the TUC put as much trust in one another as rutting stags. Agnostics accuse Christians of providing pap for the people; Christians accuse Marxists of crimes against the individual; Marxists accuse everyone who is not a Marxist of being a Fascist pig. Youngsters denigrate 'old squares', and 'old squares', in their turn, fulminate about long hair, pop stars and scruffy denims. Television, radio and the newspapers love to stir it up – to highlight mistrust and the legacies of mistrust – because, in their pragmatic opinion, such 'scandals' help the viewing, listening and circulation figures.

I believe that politicians, aided and abetted by the news media, have gradually turned us all into a confusion of quarrelling mobs. When it suits their argument, standards are turned upside down and inside out. Political commentators have begun to regard a man's 'word of honour' as a sick joke. Cynical gossip columnists have begun to hold up as examples of probity and worth people who cheat the taxman (and, therefore, all other taxpayers), who scoff at religious observances (and, therefore, at the foundations of a caring society) and who, by public exhibitions of sexual promiscuity, cause pain and misery to their marriage partners and to their children. Is it any wonder that ordinary folk, whose instinctive desire has always been to live in amity with their neighbours, have begun to behave unethically themselves, in a pathetic effort at self-defence? Is it any wonder that the only standard which seems to be considered important today is that of material possession?

The Padre and Donald had few material possessions. They were both aware of human weakness and neither placed himself above it. But they recognized that in order to enjoy a good life standards of integrity had to be maintained. So they maintained them, without question, and never doubted that others, given the chance, would also do so.

In simple innocence? Or in wise recognition of the truth that the divinity in every man is worthy of love and respect.

4

In the Stranger's Guise

Fifty years ago in the Manse, we had no radio or television, no car, no pocket-money, no school meals, no organized games – in short, none of the advantages which children of today take for granted. And yet we had plenty 'going for us', because our parents and a few other like-minded adults helped and encouraged us to do many things for ourselves.

Such also was the situation of the tinkers and tramps who made Southend a happy hunting-ground. Though unable – or unwilling – to command official benefits of any kind, they lived comfortably enough within their own terms, because people were kind to them and offered help (remembering St Columba's *Rune of Hospitality*: 'Give to the stranger . . . because often comes the Christ in a stranger's guise') and encouraged them as well to practise the crafts and trades inherited over the centuries from their kith and kin.

The word tinker has an honourable origin. In old Scots it is 'tinkler', meaning simply a tin worker – someone who makes a tinkling sound as he applies the tools of his trade. In the past century it has acquired a nuance of derogation – like the word 'nigger' – and social workers now insist that tinkers should be called 'travelling people'.

In my childhood, the majority of tinkers slept in smokey tents. The ones we knew (we still know their descendants) were called either Townsley or Williamson. A tale is told that the Townsleys can trace descent from Huguenot refugees who, in the late seventeenth century, emigrated from the Low Countries to the East Neuk of Fife in search of tolerance. The Williamsons may constitute the remnant of a clan group rendered 'homeless and landless' after Culloden.

They moved their goods and chattels from sheltered site to sheltered site in rickety handcarts often manufactured from discarded grocery boxes and old pram and bicycle wheels. At times they earned money by thinning turnips, working in the harvest fields and digging potatoes. As a rule, however, they simply wandered from house to house in the parish begging for 'auld claes' and 'a wee puckle tea an' sugar', offering to repair pots and pans (as a gesture to their ancestral trade) and displaying for sale baskets, table-mats and clothes-pegs, all of which they had made themselves. They spoke a language of their own, which we understood derived from Romany, and never mixed with us in any social sense.

We children were scared of them. When we met on the road, and they addressed us in a gabbled mixture of Romany and English, we made polite acknowledgement but immediately scuttled past and away. On Fair Days in Campbeltown they often got drunk and quarrelled and fought amongst themselves, and when they appeared in court Sheriff MacMaster Campbell would talk to them in terms of dreadful retribution and then either admonish them or fine them half a crown. But, to my knowledge, a tinker never molested or assaulted anybody who was not a tinker.

We heard lurid tales of incest and inbreeding among their number; and, indeed, in a physical sense, they were inclined to be degenerate, many of them suffering from pulmonary diseases and spinal deformities. I retain a pathetic memory of an adolescent tinker boy, gangling, vacant-faced, six feet tall, laughing and running and dragging behind him across the shore a toy horse, belonging to Jock, which Jean had given him. Some of the braggart 'lads of the village' used to tell us gaping boys how they had been challenged by blonde tinker girls to prove their manhood; but, again to my knowledge, not even the lustiest farm-hand ever accepted such invitations. The 'tinker smell', generated by wood-smoke and unwashed bodies, was an

inhibiter of normal sexual desire. In any case, the social barrier
remained too wide even for casual crossings.

The tinkers were – and still are – 'a race apart'. The Padre
always stopped on the road to talk to them, and frequently
they brought their babies to the Manse to be christened. They
did this, he suspected, in order to 'keep in' with my mother and
Maimie, who had been brought up in the ancient Highland
belief that when a tinker (or any stranger) comes to the door he
must never be turned away empty-handed. But it was his creed
that no matter what the circumstances might be, if his services
as a minister were requested it was his duty not to withhold
them.

He was never asked to officiate at a tinker wedding or a tinker
funeral. On such occasions they followed customs and carried
out rituals of their own. Each time we go to Glasgow by car
Jean and I see a tinker's grave by the roadside near Lochgair.
There is another on the Dunoon road, not far from the Glen
Croe junction.

The sad fact is that with the coming of the Welfare State the
position of tinkers has hardly changed. They are given every
chance to integrate with the wider community. They are offered
housing and settled education for their children. They receive
social security. Well-meaning people supply them with the
means to start up small businesses. But they refuse to live in
houses, preferring the nomadic outdoor life of their forbears.
Their children are moved from school to school, learning little.
They squander their dole money on drink. The great social
barrier remains almost as impregnable as before.

In our district a few young male tinkers have taken jobs on
the roads and in the shipyard in Campbeltown. They have
married girls who are not tinkers, live permanently in council
houses and appear to be creating new lives for themselves. But
in general the 'travelling people' still roam the roads with their
tents and their handcarts. Their physical health has not greatly
improved. Drunkenly they still quarrel and fight among
themselves.

Why?

Sometimes articles appear in the press, and television programmes are broadcast, which accuse the community in general and certain councils in particular, of 'neglecting' the tinkers.

One tinker whom I know personally has told newspaper and television interviewers that 'nobody does anything for the travelling people', when in fact the local council and local individuals have done everything possible to make life easier for himself and his family. He simply gave the answer which he guessed the interviewers wanted and omitted to mention a number of factors relevant to his situation.

Twice he was placed by the authorities in a good house and in a good job but on both occasions he ultimately rejected them. A local lady, whose life is dedicated to the care of tinkers, supplied him with a caravan and the facilities to learn a country craft, but in the end he rejected her kindness, too. A local farmer offered him work at the going agricultural rate, but after a day or two he gave it up, deciding apparently that life was easier on 'the dole'.

This newspaper and television 'star' also failed to point out that he is visited regularly by Willie Webb, the tinkers' Padre employed by the Church of Scotland, who can move mountains to help those members of his scattered congregation who will accept his help. Nor did he make any reference to the care devoted to himself and his family by local doctors and nurses, who are sometimes appalled but never deterred by the insanitary conditions in which, at times, they have to tend their tinker patients.

Nobody I know turns his back on a tinker. Jean spends her life attending to their wants, as she has done since she was a girl on her father's farm half a century ago. Elderly female tinkers address her by her Christian name and wear her discarded skirts and jumpers as they travel to and from Campbeltown by bus. I wage with her a running battle to prevent male tinkers acquiring my winter golfing wear, which, though admittedly somewhat tatty, remains comfortable to use.

At every house in the parish 'auld claes' and 'a wee puckle tea

an' sugar' are still supplied, even though on a basis of social
security benefits the suppliers may be less well off than the
recipients. There is no animus against the 'travelling people',
simply a recognition that their attitude to life is different and that
gratitude from them – in practical terms at any rate – is not to
be expected.

For what it's worth my answer to the problem is this. The
tinkers want to remain tinkers. They find houses cramping,
disciplined jobs frustrating. They are glad to accept charity, but
such charity must have no strings attached. Their desire is to be
free, following an old way of life. The greatest kindness we can
show them, in my opinion, is to take them as they are, to give
reasonable help when they ask for help but at other times to
leave them alone to work out their own destiny.

After all, they are not numbers on a social register, marked
with an asterisk, but human beings entitled to a freedom of
choice within the law.

Unlike the tinkers, who had their tents, the tramps we knew
slept in barns or in caves. It was a perennial disappointment to
us that they considered the Manse barn an unsuitable lodging
because it contained no warm and comfortable straw. But they
came regularly to our back door to canvas their 'trades' and to
suggest that 'a wee cup o' tea' might be acceptable. Between
tinkers and tramps, my mother and Maimie presided over a
permanent running buffet.

In summer Old Fernie roamed the woods and plantations,
uprooting and potting varieties of ferns and selling them from
door to door. His plants were delicate and moistly fresh, ideal
decorations for glass-fronted porches and 'best-room' windows.
Unless carefully tended they would last only for a season; but
when renewal time came round Old Fernie would be back with
younger and even more exotic specimens for sale. Clearly his
business philosophy resembled that of the modern car industry,
which preaches that a high sales turnover depends on inbuilt
obsolescence.

When we knew him, Fernie was about sixty years old, wrinkled, permanently in need of a shave. Once, when Archie quizzed him, he admitted that he had never shaved but that each day, with a rusty pair of scissors which he used for trimming fern-plants, he cut his greying beard 'to the bone', as he described it.

When he could procure them from satisfied 'customers' he favoured thick tweed trousers, tied in agricultural fashion just below the knee, and heavy boots, fastened not with the soft and poor quality laces of today but with the heavy leather thongs popular with farm-workers fifty years ago. Even in warm weather he liked to wear long coats, belted at the waist with rope or string. For one whole season he sported a khaki trench-coat which had belonged to the Padre in Salonika. With a gleam in his bright green eyes he would tell our neighbours that he was 'clothed in sanctity'. But as he appeared to sleep in his beloved coat as well as work in it during the day, by the end of that summer the odour of his sanctity was extremely pungent.

He was an introvert of sober habits. I never remember him taking a drink too many, and his only passion seemed to be for 'pan-drops', a few of which he always carried loose in his overflowing pockets. When he offered us one – sometimes he did this in lieu of discount after my mother had bought some of his ferns – we would accept it gladly, ignoring the fact that it was generally smeared with earth and fungus and covered in fragments of cigarette-ends.

We never discovered Fernie's real name nor any of his personal history. He spoke to us mainly about happenings in the parish – always in a slightly humorous way – and about his ferns. I think he loved his ferns more than he did human beings. He could tell us the Latin names of the different varieties – I wish I could remember them now – and describe the kind of soil in which each of them grew best. What intrigued us, however, was that to many of his specimens he gave personal names. For example a sonsy hart's tongue might be 'Big Sandy', a delicate maiden-hair 'Wee Jeannie'. Sitting with us in the barn, waiting

like a bedraggled lord for his tea to be brought to him by
Maimie, he would stroke them and speak to them and explain
from which part of the woods he had taken them.

Long ago, on the braeside north of Donald MacLean's
cottage, three sizeable 'craters' were excavated to provide
material for bottoming the main road. Now they are filled in
and camouflaged with earth, grass, trees and vegetation of all
kinds; but their outlines remain clear. Old Fernie called them
respectively the drawing-room, the dining-room and the kitchen. From the drawing-room came his Wee Jeannies, from the
dining-room his Big Sandys. In the kitchen, he told us, he found
less desirable specimens, which he dubbed 'the servants'.

Such imaginative flights appealed to us, and we would help
and encourage him to spin improbable yarns about his fern
people. Once, however, when I put forward the idea of a coy
romance between a Wee Jeannie and a Big Sandy, he became
unaccountably morose and refused to speak to us any more
that day.

On the basis of the evidence available we began to create
backgrounds for Old Fernie.

Archie was convinced he was a well-educated 'aristocrat' who
had lost all his money. Didn't he know Latin and talk, not
about parlours and 'best rooms' as did the people of Southend,
but about drawing-rooms and dining-rooms – and servants?
Willie, more of a realist, thought he might have been a gardener
who had robbed his master and spent a long time in jail.

As a future story-teller, I was inclined to favour Archie's
fancy but took pains to add a twist to it. In his youth, I suggested, he had been turned down by the girl he loved – which
would account for his sudden moroseness when romance was
mentioned – and thereafter had decided to spurn society and
live close to nature instead.

We never did discover the truth. One autumn Old Fernie
went away to wherever he used to spend the winters. He didn't
come back. He passed out of our lives like a migrating swallow.
Or – more truly, perhaps – like a character in a one-act play.

Another tramp about whose origins and background we had scanty knowledge was a small, wiry, cheerful, sardonic, sometimes gloriously inebriated man who, though most unlike a dignified Womble of Wimbledon, still rejoiced in the name of Tobermory – because, as we were led to believe, he had been born in Tobermory in the Isle of Mull.

His domicile in Southend, during many summers, was the big sea-smoothed cave beyond the graveyard at Keil, where Flora MacCambridge and the young James Ranald MacDonald had found refuge after the siege of Dunaverty. There, on a quiet evening, he could often be heard singing as he brewed a cup of tea on a driftwood fire. He owned two canvas bags with leather shoulder straps. The larger one contained his bedding and cooking utensils, the other the tools of his trade as an itinerant saw-sharpener.

The Padre, as has been shown, was a violent man with a saw. Tobermory, therefore, found him a regular customer. They talked about religion in a desultory way; but since Tobermory was inclined to sneer at the Kirk and deride its black-coated, 'respectable' image, their discussions seldom progressed beyond the stage of a few brittle generalities. Clearly Tobermory had a chip on his shoulder, and the Padre, though he himself had chips on both his shoulders, would stump away, muttering about people who refused to understand and make allowances. (The pot, we thought, calling the kettle black. But we remained firmly on the Padre's side.) Tobermory would glance after him, grin, spit out a stream of tobacco juice on the barn floor and resume work with his pliers on the teeth of our cross-cut.

At the appropriate time Maimie would come and tell him that his meal was ready. He would follow her into the kitchen, seat himself close to the glowing range and noisily consume large bowls of tea and, as often as not, cold chicken sandwiches. Then he would smoke a cigarette and exchange banter with Maimie in crudely mixed Gaelic and English.

Perhaps because of the Gaelic, my mother and Maimie seemed to like him well enough. Archie, Willie and I didn't.

Old Fernie conversed with us as equals. Tobermory talked down to us, making us feel uncomfortable by cracking jokes at the expense of our youthful inexperience.

Sometimes I concealed resentment and went to visit him. People who didn't know him may find it hard to believe, but during the summer a weekly newspaper was delivered to Tobermory in his cave, by bus from Campbeltown. I became very interested in that newspaper. It was called the *Worker*.

Reared on the bland Tory diet offered at that time by the *Glasgow Herald* – and without radio or television to suggest more uncomfortable points of view – I found that the articles in Tobermory's paper made me feel both excited and guilty. It was like turning over a smooth, beautifully marked stone only to discover underneath rotting vegetation and crawling creatures like worms and slaters. I thought of my father's congregation, dominated by the Dowager Duchess of Argyll and numerous 'well-bein' ' farmers and tradesmen. I thought of the tinkers and the tramps and the people of 'Teapot Lane' in the village who lived 'on the parish' and never went to church.

Tobermory would sit on his haunches, brewing up tea on his fire at the mouth of the cave and watching me read. Partially concealed by lowered lids, his eyes would be cunning. A smile would twist his narrow mouth. I never discussed the articles with him; he never tried to discuss them with me. When I put the paper down and bade him good-bye he would laugh and spit and perhaps make a sour comment about my innocence.

My mother would have been horrified had she known what I was doing. The Padre's reaction might have been less fraught, but, to be safe, I kept my knowledge of the *Worker* to myself. I hated what I read. It told me that as a privileged person (in a moral sense) I was blind and ignorant, that there was another, infinitely ugly side to the shining moon. It also posed a question: what are you going to do about it? The question caused me pain, because I felt unarmed and inadequate. It is a feeling that has never left me.

I wondered if it troubled Tobermory? I think possibly it did, because when he had accumulated sufficient money from the sharpening of saws he often went on a wild alcoholic binge which was the wonder – and, in some cases, the envy – of the people of Southend. Obviously it was his way of forgetting something.

One summer night my father was coming home after visiting a friend in the village. Dusk had fallen. As he tramped up the steep Machrimore Brae, not far from the Manse, he saw something on the summit – something silhouetted against the moonlit sky – which made him shiver. In the middle of the road was a lumpy mass which might have been a body. Round it a tattered creature leaped and swung, uttering cries. Vague intimations of black magic assailed the Padre. He moved closer, then stopped to listen, desperately trying to remember the Gaelic incantation which offered protection from the evil eye.

Gradually the cries were translated into a kind of music and the music into badly articulated words, which, nevertheless, my father could understand: 'Jean MacNeill's in love wi' me, I'm as happy as can be! How wad ye like if you were me? Fal-di-riddle-i-doh!' With some relief he recognized Tobermory, crazily drunk, dancing round his canvas bags.

Tobermory sensed his approach. As he reached the crest of the brae Tobermory stopped singing, pirouetted rapidly on one foot, then fell heavily on top of the bags and became violently sick.

Machrimore Brae was a long mile from the cave at Keil, so the Padre shouldered Tobermory's bags and, amid bouts of vomiting, helped him to reach the Manse barn and bed down for the night.

In the morning Tobermory was gone. But a few days later he was back, spry and sardonic as ever, touting for work.

As far as we were concerned, as children, Old Fernie and Tobermory emerged from limbo and eventually returned to it. Peter the Jostler was different. We knew his full name, Peter McArthur. We knew he had been nicknamed the Jostler because it was his habit, caught in a crowd, to shoulder and push a way out of it, as if his life depended on winning free. We knew that he had been a miner. We knew that his strange ways were the result of his having been involved in a pit accident and trapped underground for many hours.

Peter was not a summer visitor like other tramps. He was always with us, roaming from house to house in Kintyre, as if searching for something.

To anyone who didn't know him his appearance and behaviour were bizarre, even frightening. If presented with an old coat he usually put it on at once, on top of a grisly collection of other garments. In consequence he looked grotesque, a Michelin-man scarecrow. But what fascinated us even more – and what caused us cruel, giggling amusement – was his continual fear of being 'jammed'.

On being invited into a house, he would carefully examine the walls of the room – usually the kitchen – in which he was to be entertained. Then he would take a chair, test the strength of its legs with powerful hands and finally place it with its back to the wall, as far from the fire as possible. If his examinations and tests proved satisfactory he would sit down, still looking around him suspiciously, and await attention. If they didn't he would proceed backwards out of the room and the house, muttering through a dirty, unkempt beard that he was being 'jammed'.

Soup or tea had to be served to him in a plain white bowl. If offered a decorated bowl or a teacup with markings on it he was immediately 'jammed' and would effect a quick escape, uttering baleful sounds. My mother and Maimie, knowing him well, made few mistakes. The Manse kitchen, therefore, was one of his favourite stopping-places. Peering round a door-jamb, we often saw him sitting there after having had a good lunch, dozing in his chair while the minutes passed towards tea-time. On such occasions Maimie would go about her business quietly, and my mother would postpone an ironing session, because if Peter awoke to find a red-hot iron in his vicinity he would be grievously 'jammed' and a temporary peace would be broken.

Archie and Willie and I were never allowed to go near him.

The village children had a habit of shouting after him as he padded along the road: 'Tak' the hens oot o' yer pockets!' This oblique – and unfounded – accusation of theft infuriated him, and he would heave large stones at them in retaliation. The sight of us in the kitchen might have triggered off a similar bout of mayhem.

My father was apt to 'jam' him, too. At the beginning he had tried to speak to Peter, but nothing coherent ever issued from behind the bedraggled beard, and it seemed that the Padre's offer of spiritual comfort was either not understood or deliberately declined.

Some people were able to get through to him by means of a dram, under the influence of which he might be persuaded to sing a stave or two of a Scots song. He had a reasonable bass voice, roughened and sometimes made to waver by bronchial phlegm.

He was unpopular with the rabbit-catchers. Sometimes, during his wanderings, if he came across a rabbit in a snare, he would catch it, calm it with gentle hands, loosen the wire about its body and allow it to lope away. Hiding behind a bush or under the lip of a bunker on the golf-course, we often saw him do it. We would laugh together as he remained on his knees, staring after the released animal, a motionless heap of ragged garments black against the short green grass. We would shout insults at him, then flee with careless agility as he made stiff and ponderous efforts to rise and pursue us. Eventually, when the opportunity occurred, we would tell the tale to Dan, our favourite rabbit-catcher, who would swear and describe the Jostler as 'a bloody menace'. Our childish, undeveloped imaginations failed to glimpse the truth: to him the rabbits were 'jammed'; to him no living creature deserved such agony.

One morning he was found lying under a whin bush on a braeside not far from Campbeltown. Soaking wet, stiff as a log, he was taken to the Poor House hospital, where, without regaining consciousness, he died. They buried him at Kilkerran, in the town cemetery, in the place reserved for paupers.

Today it is likely that Peter the Jostler would be looked after by the State. Would he be any happier, confined and regimented in a geriatric hospital? Would psychiatrists discover a cure for his terrible malaise, or would their probings result in his being shut away in a mental home?

We saw him at the time as a subject for hidden laughter. Now, understanding what he must have suffered, 'jammed' in a collapsing pit-shaft, I find his memory infinitely sad. Did anybody care? My mother and Maimie did. So did many other housewives in the parish. But what about the rest of us?

produce and buy goods in Glasgow. In those days such a journey must have been a sea-faring Everest. He had an eye for the girls – at any rate before he married – and though my father was inclined to gloss over this aspect of his personality I have an idea that I may have more blood relations in the islands than are recorded in the family bibles.

But it was Old Angus's attitude to the Sabbath that intrigued me most. I imagined that my ancestors had always possessed an outlook on religion that was bleak and sad, especially on Sundays. In Old Angus's young days, at the beginning of last century, this was far from being the truth. Before and after morning service he and his young friends used to enjoy such sports as the long jump and putting the stone. Business transactions were common on a Sunday afternoon, even among Kirk elders.

The services themselves were not sacrosanct. On one occasion, as the minister announced the text of his sermon, a boy came rushing into the church with the news that whales had appeared in a neighbouring bay. Shouting apologies, Old Angus and the rest of the congregation rose in a body and ran off to launch their boats. All the minister could do was to follow them and spend the rest of the afternoon watching his flock driving the whales towards the shore with sticks and stones, so that they might be left high and dry when the tide receded.

'A work of necessity and mercy,' my father would point out, unctuously. 'Tender whale meat was a change from salt beef that was always stringy and tough. Not only could the blubber be rendered down for lamp-oil, it was also a useful food. I remember a North Uist proverb which went something like this: "*Is math am biadh femanaich aran seagail agus roin.*" ("Good food it is for a seaweed worker, rye bread and blubber.")'

I suppose the truth was that if the Roman Catholics could spend their Sunday afternoons in profitable and enjoyable pursuits, some Protestants were unwilling to stand aside and let them have all the fun.

Following the Disruption, however, happy-go-lucky Sabbaths

were gradually displaced by the doom and gloom which so
many Sassenachs believe, mistakenly, to be characteristic of the
Church of Scotland. The pendulum swung from 'the broad way',
which was how the seceders described my great-grandfather's
attitude, to the 'straight and narrow'.

Indeed, the new road became so narrow as to be almost
impassable. One Sunday, on his way to church, Old Angus met
the Free Church minister on the road. He touched his cap: 'A
fine day,' he said. The tall black figure stopped, fixed him with
an eagle eye and thundered: 'This is not a day, Angus, to be
speaking of days!'

When he was inducted to the parish of Southend in 1910, the
Padre found that its religious history was not unlike that of his
native island.

He spoke to old men whose parents had been alive at the end
of the eighteenth and at the beginning of the nineteenth centuries, old men who could tell stories about Communion
Sundays when tents were erected around the Kirk for the supply
of food, sweetmeats and drink and in which children could be
looked after while their fathers and mothers attended the long
services. It was like a fair, they told him: a Holy Fair, perhaps,
in the Burnsian sense. But as time went on the climate of
religious opinion changed. In Southend, as in North Uist, all
the joy went out of it, and I have a notion that King David,
who danced before the Lord, might have thought as little of the
encompassing 'blackness' as my brothers and I did.

Surely it is a good thing that happier Sundays have now, once
more, become the rule rather than the exception. After all, as I
understand it, Christ died to make us happy. Is the Sabbath not
the most appropriate day of all to enjoy leisure and to be
'speaking of days'?

But the bitterness engendered by the Disruption in North
Uist was as nothing compared with that caused by the eviction
of innocent people from their crofts in order to make way for
'the great Cheviot'.

During the Clearances in the Highlands and Islands, when

absentee landlords – many of them living in England – autho-
rized their local representatives to get rid of 'unprofitable'
crofters and fill their estates with 'profitable' sheep, some of the
seeds were sown of present-day Scottish Nationalism. With the
thatch of their 'black houses' burning, with their wives and
children blood-stained from beatings with soldiers' musket-
butts and policemen's batons, with tattered plaids as their only
protection from winter cold, with ranting clergymen (whose
stipends were often paid by the landlords) preaching submission
to God's will, with no help in sight from Government or from
fat, 'I'm all right, Jack' farming neighbours in the south, the
crofters of the Highlands and Islands were struck by a bitterness
whose breath is still strong.

The Clearances began in the counties of Sutherland and Ross
in the second half of the eighteenth century, notoriously on
estates owned by the Duke of Sutherland. Their full evil came
to North Uist early in the nineteenth century, when Britain was
recovering from the long Napoleonic wars and the demand for
meat – and especially for mutton – had become even stronger
than before. Then, as on the mainland, the sad cries of the
evicted people of Sollas were overcome by the bleatings of
many sheep.

On the face of it, North Uist had a thriving kelp industry. The
people, however, remained poor, and even before the actual
physical violence of the Clearances some of them had been
forced to give up the struggle and quit the island of their
fathers. Crofter rents were screwed higher and higher to
screaming point. Those who worked at the seaweed, collecting
it, spreading it out to dry and then burning it in a kiln to make
kelp, were paid thirty shillings per ton for their industry while
the landlord made a profit of some £18 on the same amount. No
wonder the bard Ian MacCodrum made a protest:

> Look around you and see the gentry
> With no pity for the poor creatures,
> With no kindness to their kin.

They do not think that you belong to the land,
And although they leave you empty
They do not see it as a loss.
They have lost their respect
For every law and promise
That was among the men
Who took their land from the foe.

But poetic protests fell with no more impact than confetti on
leather-hard consciences. Many of my ancestors in North Uist,
rack-rented into poverty, emigrated voluntarily to America and
Australia. Others became vagrants, wandering southwards to
Glasgow and the Lowlands, where, if they were lucky, they
found menial work. Some of the young men became soldiers,
fighting for officers who would later callously evict their families
and for a Britain which, having used them in battle, would then
cast them aside with as little concern as if they were spent
matches.

Forced evictions began in North Uist in 1841, when Duncan
Shaw, not only Sheriff Substitute in the Long Island but also
factor for the North Uist Estates (how's that for legal impar-
tiality?), recommended to a Select Committee appointed to
inquire into the condition of the population of the Highlands
and Islands that 2500 people in North Uist, out of a total of
4600, should be removed to Canada. His master, the owner of
North Uist (and of other property in Skye) was Godfrey
William Wentworth Macdonald, fourth Baron of the Isles, and
a descendant of the Macdonald chiefs of Sleat.

According to Old Angus, Lord Macdonald was at heart a
decent enough man who did his best to alleviate destitution in
the island, especially during the potato famine of 1846. But it
seems he was heavily in debt – some say to the tune of nearly
£200000 – and the pressures on him to use 'the great Cheviot'
as a means of restoring his fortunes were as great as those on
less humane landowners. Finally, he, too, was petitioning for '*an
armed force to enable the constituted authorities to compel the
people to give obedience to the law*'.

The flash-point of the North Uist Clearances occurred in 1849, when it was decided to evict all the Sollas tenantry on the plea that they were in arrears of rent. Old Angus was a young man at the time and witnessed some of the almost incredible barbarity committed in the name of so-called law and order. As a boy, listening at the peat-fire, the Padre heard stories from the *bodach*'s own lips. He, in turn, told them to me. I will try, however, to be objective and to rely on recorded history, rather more than on legend, for the facts, though such objectivity – and such justice – was never employed by Lord Macdonald in dealing with the people of Sollas. (Nor by his ancestors in the sixteenth century, when, by offering a Judas hand of friendship, they captured and killed four MacVicar brothers in North Uist and took over their lands.)

Sollas is a square mile of flat, treeless country in the north end of the island, bounded on the west by a tidal beach of white sand and enclosed in a kind of trough between sand-blown dunes and the lower slopes of the inland hills. Though exposed to fierce Atlantic weather, the land is kind, possibly the best in the island, and in 1849 600 people lived there in the townships of Dunskellar, Malaglate, Middlequarter and Sollas itself. They were for the most part Macdonalds, with a deep love for every bare inch of their homeland.

Lord Macdonald's commissioner, Patrick Cooper, claimed that the soil was unsuited for small tenants and incapable of improvement by drainage. (Fifty years later this claim was proved to be wrong when the Congested Districts Board divided the farm of Sollas into twelve successful crofts.) On the other hand, he said, the ground provided ideal grazing for sheep. In the month of May, therefore, on behalf of Lord Macdonald, he offered to overlook the crofters' arrears of rent and to ship them all, with their families, to Canada.

Shocked and saddened by this proposal, the tenants of Sollas attempted to organize opposition. Their spokesman pointed out that the potato crop for the previous three years had failed but that they could tide over this difficult period if Lord

Macdonald would offer them employment by way of kelp-making or drainage.

But the land-owner (or his commissioner) had made up his mind. Employing what was in effect a con trick, Patrick Cooper now told the tenants that Lord Macdonald would pay all their passage money. When the offer was examined in detail, however, they found that the money was to come from the sale of their own effects, with no allowance made for their buildings.

Finally, a writ was granted for the eviction of the Sollas people.

On Saturday 14 July the first attempt to execute it was made by Sheriff Officer Roderick Macdonald and two assistants. They were driven from Malaglate by a barrage of stones.

They tried again two days later, this time accompanied by Sheriff Substitute Shaw, Patrick Cooper and twenty policemen. The same thing happened.

A third try was made on 17 July, when Cooper, sensing that he was a main source of the crofters' anger, absented himself. As the party approached Malaglate it was confronted by a crowd of 300 men, women and children. Roderick Macdonald, the Sheriff Officer, said afterwards that warning signals were flying: 'Namely a pole with some black thing on it, but I couldn't say whether it was a flag or a bonnet. The first flag was about fifty yards from the house, and three flags were on top of a hill about a mile distant. The crowd said they would not allow us to go on with the removals. They did not strike, but were speaking, and said that if we attempted the removals we should see the consequences.' Sheriff Substitute Shaw was troubled. He had no enthusiasm for his task, and when the rain came on he became even more unhappy. He ordered a retreat to Lochmaddy.

From Armadale Castle in Skye Lord Macdonald now wrote to the Home Secretary, asking for 'an armed force' to deal with his recalcitrant tenants. But his answer was a dusty one. He was told that before the military were sent the law should employ 'the county force only'.

On 1 August an all-Inverness-shire party consisting of Sheriff Substitute Shaw, Sheriff Substitute Colquhoun, Procurator Fiscal Mackay, Commissioner Patrick Cooper, Factor James Thomas Macdonald, Superintendent MacBean, and thirty-three constables advanced on Sollas. Accompanying the party were two men who might be described as neutral observers – 'Our Own Reporter' from the *Inverness Courier* and the Rev. Finlay MacRae, parish minister of North Uist. (The majority of the people of Sollas belonged to the Free Church, but at this particular time, inexplicably, their own minister seems to have been absent.) Again the crofters and their families had gathered in a tight crowd on the *machair*. Again black, defiant flags were flying. Again it was raining.

The first few hours of the confrontation were spent in argument, with the Rev. Finlay MacRae acting as mediator. On the word of the *Inverness Courier* reporter, the crofters were 'in such a state of excitement that it appeared more than questionable, should an ejectment be proceeded with, whether a promise made to Mr MacRae in the morning that no resistance would be made to the officers, would be fulfilled'.

The day went on. So did the rain. As people became wetter and colder they also became more surly and hot-tempered. Patrick Cooper shouted to the crofters, demanding that they should accept the writ and emigrate. The minister and Superintendent MacBean 'added their arguments and advices in Gaelic'. Eventually four or five families agreed to leave, but the remainder stubbornly refused. According to Old Angus's story the men were quiet and peaceable enough: the women were more militant, screaming abuse at the police in general and at Patrick Cooper in particular.

As dusk began to fall Sheriff Substitute Colquhoun and Superintendent MacBean, both mainland men without much stomach for island weather, decided to withdraw. Before doing so, however, they made a quick move to assert their authority. Policemen charged forward and, after a short, angry struggle, were able to handcuff two men and drag them out of the crowd.

The men were Roderick MacPhail and Archibald Maclean, the latter being related by blood to the MacVicars.

After the 'gentry' and the constables had left for Lochmaddy, the *Courier* reporter, like a good professional, remained behind to interview the crofters. Their argument was that there was no need for emigration: 'If Lord Macdonald would increase the crofts to double the present size for which there is sufficient improvable land, and would give leases and encouragement to improvements, we would be content to pay rents, and we would have seaware and stock sufficient.'

Next morning the authorities reached Malaglate by ten o'clock, hoping that the arrests they had made the night before would have had a salutary effect on the inhabitants. But though this time the people themselves remained indoors, black flags were again flying. The sight of them triggered off an outbreak of the violence that had been simmering evilly beneath the wind and the rain of the past twenty-four hours.

With no more discussion, no more argument, the police took up positions along the main track through Malaglate. The Sheriffs asked a question at the door of each house: 'Are you willing to emigrate on the terms offered?' If the answer was no – and almost invariably it was – then the constables proceeded with the work of demolition. Thatch was torn off the roofs; clothes, bedding, spinning-wheels, fish-barrels, tables and benches were hurled out into the open and the house-timbers stripped for burning. Patrick Cooper, surrounded by constables, himself supervised each eviction.

As the destruction went on, the neighbouring crofters of Dunskellar, Middlequarter and Sollas gathered on an adjacent knoll, underneath one of the black flags. They watched as the Malaglate folk, at first in grim silence, were subjected to indignities. Then suddenly – and this is one of Old Angus's stories – the wife of a man called John MacAskill, a weaver with nine children, emerged from her 'black house' with a child in her arms, calling out: *'Tha mo chlann air a bhi air am murt!'* ('My children are being murdered!') The watching crofters could endure it no longer. They rushed down towards the township, brandishing sticks and stones.

The police were instructed to draw truncheons. Superintendent MacBean approached the crowd. He 'explained what the men were actually doing in the house. He was listened to quietly; but as he returned a stone was thrown at him, and he had scarcely joined his men when a heavy volley of stones drove the assistant from the roof of the house, and a band of from fifty to one hundred women, with a few men and boys, came running up from the shore, shouting and armed with large stones, with which they compelled the assistants to fall back behind the police for shelter. Fresh supplies of large, sharp-pointed stones were obtained from the bed of a small stream, and several heavy volleys were discharged, most of them, however, falling short of the officers.'

The police were now formed into two divisions and ordered to attack the crowd. One division charged the women from the rear, the other on the flank. The women attempted to stand their ground, but the flailing truncheons were too much for them. They retreated first along the *machair*, then across the white shore, screaming and scratching and calling out to their less gallant men: 'Be manly and help us!' Their clothes were torn, their heads and arms bruised and bloody from the impact of truncheons and fists.

Early in the afternoon Superintendent MacBean called off the running battle. The constables returned to Malaglate. The defeated but still defiant women again gathered on the knoll to tend one another's wounds and to shout more insults. Old Angus retained a keen Gaelic memory of much of what they said. So did the reporter from the *Inverness Courier*, who later wrote that the maddened women were soon uttering 'such wishes as that their men might come down and wash their hands in their enemies' hearts-blood, and that the devil and his angels might come and sweep them out of the land'.

The men of Sollas were slow to make any heroic response, believing perhaps that their families might suffer less if they refused to meet violence with violence. Once or twice some adolescents of both sexes advanced on the police to throw stones and then run away.

Patrick Cooper found the situation difficult.

A further attempt to destroy the houses of Malaglate, he suspected, might spark off a physical battle in which the women of Sollas would at last be joined by their men-folk. If that happened, greatly outnumbered as the authorities were, death might come to the *machair* – death which would almost certainly include his own.

There was another complication. Sheriff Substitute Colquhoun had become sickened by the police brutality and, as a result, was refusing to serve any more writs, claiming that there were faults in the wording of them.

Furthermore, the Rev. Finlay MacRae was preaching less violence and more understanding of the people's plight.

Cooper decided that if they made ten token ejectments and took a few prisoners his party could then retire to Lochmaddy without losing too much face.

Two Malaglate crofters, Archibald Boyd and Roderick MacCuish (MacCuish was another relative of the MacVicars) were pursued to the shore, beaten up by the police, arrested and handcuffed. The ejectments then continued.

'The ninth ejectment was that of a family in Middlequarter, named Monk, who had taken an active part in all the previous opposition to the authorities. It was found necessary to remove the women by force. One of them threw herself on the ground, and either fell or pretended to fall into hysterics – (fortunately I have not had experience enough to know the difference) – uttering the most doleful sounds, and barking and yelping like a dog for five or ten minutes. Another, with many tears, sobs and groans, put up a petition to the Sheriffs that they would leave the roof over part of her house where she had a loom with cloth in it which she was weaving; and a third woman, the eldest, made such an attack with a stick on an officer, and missing her blow, sprung upon him and knocked off his hat.

Two stout policemen had difficulty in carrying her to the door.'

Meanwhile the Rev. Finlay MacRae talked earnestly to the crofters. His message was that if they promised to emigrate the following year they might be allowed to occupy their houses for the winter. He talked also to Patrick Cooper, finally securing from him a promise that if the crofters agreed to sign pledges to emigrate the following year he would call off the police.

Suddenly, as evening came – and the minister continued to plead passionately with both sides – the crofters' resistance came to an end, like an Atlantic gale that blows itself out into a zephyr. The confrontation was over.

Next morning the tenants put their names to a bond, promising that they would emigrate to Canada whenever and however Lord Macdonald decided. All their stock was surrendered to Cooper at his valuation, though each family was allowed to keep a cow and a pony, the cow for milk, the pony for carrying peat. The prisoners – Roderick MacPhail, Archibald Maclean, Archibald Boyd and Roderick MacCuish – were released on bail guaranteed by the Rev. Finlay MacRae and on his word that they would surrender themselves for trial when called.

But the story of the Sollas affair was not yet finished. Indeed, its futility is still being demonstrated in the crofting history of Scotland.

On 13 September 1849 the arrested men were tried before Lord Cockburn, charged with mobbing, rioting, and obstructing and deforcing officers of the law in the execution of their duties.

In the interval between the confrontation at Sollas and the trial in Inverness public opinion had taken a curious turn. Sympathy was strong, not only for the crofters but also for Lord Macdonald, who had come to be regarded as 'the victim of events rather than the creator of them'. This would seem to support Old Angus's belief that the 'Lord of the Isles' had a decent side to him. But – I wonder? In the Highlands of a century ago a person called Macdonald was liable to be more warmly regarded than somebody with a name like – for example

– Cooper. In any case, Cooper was merely an employee of the owner of the land. President Truman had a notice in the White House: 'The buck stops here.' A similar notice would have been appropriate in Armadale Castle.

Lord Cockburn concluded his summing up of the trial with these words: 'Your duty and mine is simply to uphold the majesty of the law. . . . I have no facts before me from which to applaud Lord Macdonald or the people. I do not wish to give an opinion, and so help me God I have no opinion on the subject!'

The jury, however, were untroubled by considerations of neutrality or legality. They found the accused guilty – on the evidence they could do nothing else – but recommended them 'to the utmost leniency and mercy of the Court in consideration of the cruel, though it may be legal, proceedings adopted in ejecting the whole people of Sollas'.

The spectators in the court-room rose to their feet, shouting and clapping. Lord Cockburn silenced them. Unemotionally – but betraying a personal opinion after all? – he said he found no reason to impose severe sentences. Four months in prison for each of the accused would be enough.

Before autumn was at an end Roderick MacPhail, Archibald Maclean, Archibald Boyd and Roderick MacCuish were back in North Uist, telling the tale of their adventures to Old Angus. They were full of wonder that, in spite of every indication to the contrary, justice could still be found in the hearts of powerful men.

But now comes the irony. It may be that Lord Macdonald was reluctant to flout public opinion and send his tenants away from Sollas. Or it may be that Patrick Cooper and his henchmen were less than efficient. In the event, though in January 1850 Cooper did warn the crofters that they should get ready to leave for America, in July, when they should have gone, they were still in Sollas.

Two months later, however, to the surprise and dismay of every islander, they were suddenly removed, lock, stock and barrel, to Loch Efort, in the south of the island, where each family was given twenty acres.

The land at Loch Efort was poor and some distance from the sea. The crofters, already demoralized by uncertainty, became even more confused and unhappy. Their morale reached so low an ebb that in the end they petitioned Lord Macdonald to send them to Australia. After long months of argument he agreed to help the emigration of the young and the healthy. He would do nothing for the aged and the sick.

In December 1852 the Sollas people were herded aboard the steamer *Celt*, bound for Campbeltown, here in Kintyre. At Campbeltown they were transferred with other emigrants – some from Southend – to the frigate *Hercules*. When the *Hercules* stopped for water and mails at Queenstown, in Ireland, a number of the emigrants were found to be suffering from smallpox.

How many of the victims remembered, in their suffering, the cool breezes of Sollas?

It was all a mess, a 'muck-up': an example of what can happen when respect for individual freedom becomes a matter for contempt. No wonder, in the Highlands of Scotland today, we are suspicious of absentee landlords, of cold bureaucracy, of government from a distance. No wonder the songs of North Uist are sometimes incredibly sad.

And yet it seems to me that my great-grandfather, on the evidence of some good words he had to say about Lord Macdonald – whose family the MacVicars had no reason to love – retained a sense of proportion. So did the Padre, who was always prepared to admit that a few – if only a *very* few – of the Sollas crofters were inclined to be lazy and inefficient and that Lord Macdonald, ill served by his commissioner and lacking funds, may have been weak and vacillating rather than positively villainous. But in his Hebridean heart there continued to exist sympathy for those without money or privilege. In any argument he would almost invariably take the side of the underdog.

It may have been an ancestral instinct that prompted him, in

1929, when minister of Southend, to stand for election to the Argyll County Council against the Duke of Argyll's factor, who opposed the idea of subsidized houses for agricultural workers. Most of his parishioners rented farms from the Duke, and it was a nine days' wonder, therefore, when he won by a large majority. 'That day,' commented the *Campbeltown Courier*, 'there must have been more false faces in Southend than at Hallowe'en.' I think the faces were all true – the faces of democracy upturned against those of bland, uncaring power.

I think I have the same instinct as the Padre. All my life I have been inclined to support the meek and the humble, sometimes without cause.

It has also taken me a long time to learn how to accept favours with grace and gratitude. Even yet, realizing how privileged I am to be a son of the Manse, and remembering the agony of my forbears on Sollas, I experience pangs of guilt. I try to do my best for those denied good fortune. The question is, have I tried hard enough?

In Southend, in contrast to North Uist and other parts of the Highlands, there is no history of forced Clearances. And yet, from about 1750 to the beginning of the current century, people regularly left Southend seeking a better living in Canada, Australia, New Zealand and America. Around 1750 the population of the parish was approximately 3000. When my father became minister in 1910 it had dwindled almost to its present level of about 500.

In a paper published in 1962 by the State Department of Archives and History in North Carolina, concerning men and women from Kintyre who settled there in the years 1774–5, the following reasons are given for their emigration: 'low wages, high rents, low prices of cattle, high prices of bread due to distilling, the conversion of arable lands into sheep pastures, and the exactions of landlords'.

Around the rocky shorelands of Southend there can still be seen, grass-grown and deserted, the ruins of the townships from which some of those people came. Balmagomery, Balmac-vicar, Balimacmurchie, Balinamoil – the names are like an old song sighing down the wind. Today such places appear to be of interest only to local shepherds and to the Royal Commission on the Ancient and Historical Monuments of Scotland.

But when strangers from overseas come to visit us, sometimes an old song can acquire a new and vigorous tune.

In the summer of 1975 Mrs Harvey B. Hunter of Charlotte, North Carolina, unexpectedly dropped in to see us. She was accompanied by her daughter-in-law, a lecturer in history at the University of North Carolina.

Mrs Hunter is a formidable lady, eighty years of age, who, with the help of two sons, conducts the business of a large dairy farm. At the gate of her house, she told me – in an attractive Southern accent which I had imagined existed only in the movies – there stands the model of a cow, twenty feet high.

She and her daughter-in-law had less than three hours to spare. Could I, in that time, give her any information about her ancestor, Daniel Caldwell, who had emigrated from Southend in 1774? She showed me a copy of the testimonial to his good character which he had carried with him to America. It was signed by David Campbell, minister of Southend, and John Reid, elder.

We stood on Achnamara lawn, looking out over the sunlit bay at the Rock of Dunaverty and at the old jetty which lies close to it. American hustle is all very well, but this was ridiculous. Nevertheless, in courtesy to strangers, I exercised my brain – a notable effort immediately after lunch on a warm afternoon – and presently there came to me a story told by Jean's late father, old Willie McKerral: about people named Caldwell who had helped his own family in private distilling operations. 'Excuse me a minute,' I said.

I went into the house and rang up Jean's sister-in-law, Nellie McKerral. She and her husband possessed, I knew, some family papers which might indicate where the Caldwells had lived in

Southend. Sure enough, they did. In 1774, the Caldwell's had been tenants in the farm of Christlach.

I went back out on to the lawn, where the ladies were talking to Jean and admiring our roses. They reckoned they were better roses than they themselves could grow in North Carolina. Delighted by such evidence of American magnanimity, I cut two of the best blooms and presented them with one each.

I looked out over the bay again, at the jetty near Dunaverty, and another memory occurred to me.

'Do you know the month in 1774 when Daniel Caldwell left Southend?'

'August,' said Mrs Hunter.

'The ship he sailed in – was she by any chance the *Ulysses*?'

'Say, that was the very name! How did you know?'

I knew because I had heard of the *Ulysses* from many of the old story-tellers of Southend: how she had anchored in the bay while emigrants were taken out from the jetty beneath Dunaverty in a small boat and someone on the shore had played a lament on the bagpipes.

'Your ancestor,' I told Mrs Hunter, 'sailed for America from out there, less than half a mile from where you are standing now.'

She found words difficult. Her daughter-in-law made notes and worked hard with her camera.

'Now then,' I said, 'we'll use my car and have a look around.'

I stopped first at the graveyard at Keil, where I showed them the gravestone of John Reid, the elder who had signed Daniel Caldwell's testimonial. I told them that his descendants still lived in the parish and that a modern John Reid is a close friend of mine.

Mrs Hunter was all eyes, scrambling about the knolls and hollows of the ancient burying place like an adolescent. I admired her fitness and said so. 'I can still take a ladder and repair the roof of our chicken-run,' she announced, somewhat tartly. Her daughter-in-law took more photographs.

Then I drove them three miles north to Christlach Farm,

where Daniel Caldwell had tried to help the meagre family income by working – without much success, it appears – as a part-time shoe-maker. More photographs were taken. Mrs Hunter sighed. 'Just wait,' she said. 'Just wait till I tell them about this back home!'

Finally we went to the church: St Blaan's Kirk in the centre of the parish, in which the Padre had preached for forty-seven years. I told them it had been built in 1773 and opened for public worship early in 1774. I explained also that the pews of Norwegian pine were the original ones, unchanged for more than 200 years.

While her daughter-in-law used her camera and made still more notes, I led Mrs Hunter to a back pew. Sunlight fell on it from one of the small lead-paned windows. Its colour was golden brown. 'This is the Christlach seat,' I told her. 'The present owner of the farm still claims it. Your ancestor, Daniel Caldwell, was obviously a good church-goer, otherwise he wouldn't have got a testimonial signed by both the minister and an elder. In the early part of 1774, therefore, he must often have sat in this actual pew, before leaving in August. Come, Mrs Hunter, sit where he sat. Two hundred years doesn't seem such a long time now, does it?'

She sat carefully on the polished pine. For a long minute she said nothing, staring up at the empty pulpit. Then, quietly, she began to cry. 'Oh, my,' she said, 'this is the most wunnerful day of ma life!'

It was a wonderful day for me, too. It's not often one finds oneself in the privileged position of making another human being completely happy.

6

Upon a Sabbath Day it Fell

When we were boys at the Manse, the Sabbath was a day of discipline: but discipline often alleviated by private amusement.

Being the principal actor in the scene, with a service to conduct and a sermon to preach, the Padre spent the morning in a tense and anxious mood, like a champion boxer before a fight. During the time between breakfast – which almost invariably consisted of bacon and eggs, tea, my mother's soda scones and bramble jelly – and the moment of his entering the pulpit at mid-day, my mother and Maimie acted as his trainer and chief second, pandering to his needs both spiritual and physical. Archie and Willie and I were instructed to behave ourselves and to keep well out of his way.

We made certain that we kept out of his way, because Christian tolerance to his family was not one of the Padre's outstanding characteristics on a Sunday morning. None of us, for example, went near the bathroom at this time, because, in his opinion, a movement of the bowels was essential before good preaching, and the mood to achieve it might come upon him at any minute between ten o'clock and half past eleven.

Once, before experience shed light on the situation, Willie went to the bathroom at eleven o'clock, carefully shutting himself in by securing the small brass chain attached to the door. A few minutes later the Padre came quickly upstairs, intent upon action, and found his way to fulfilment blocked.

'Who's in there?' he thundered.

'It's me,' squeaked Willie.

'Come out at once and let me in!'

'But I'm just in the middle of – '

'Open this door!'

'But, Dadda – '

In a crisis the Padre was inclined to be impulsive. 'Blasted boy!' he roared and thrust so vigorous a shoulder at the door that the brass chain was torn from its screws. Next moment Willie was yanked off the lavatory seat (where he had been comfortably reading *Comic Cuts*) and hurled out, bare-bottomed, on to the landing. His trousers were thrown after him and the door slammed shut.

Even into old age – and not only on a Sunday – the Padre considered that a daily bowel movement (in the morning) was essential to good health. To make sure it came to him he cultivated two unvarying habits.

The first was a nightly glass of Eno's Fruit Salt. At about half past midnight, his regular bed-time, the peace of the Manse was shattered by a loud bang and double thud as he closed the outside front door and shot the rusty bolts. Then, at speed, he padded along the passage towards the kitchen and the scullery beyond, where the cold tap was turned on, a tumbler filled, the Eno's spooned in and loudly stirred. After only a short pause for drinking, the spoon was hurled with a crash into the empty tumbler. Thereafter the footsteps receded, a bedroom door banged and blessed silence fell upon the house.

As a small boy, my brother Kenneth slept in the bedroom above the kitchen with his youngest brother John. He remembers how, one night, disturbed by the usual post-midnight commotion, he waited breathlessly for the crash of the teaspoon in the tumbler. It didn't come. According to his own story he failed to sleep another wink, wondering what had happened. Subsequent delicate inquiries revealed that on this occasion the spoon had missed its target and landed softly and silently on a dishcloth which Maimie had left steeping in the sink.

The Padre's second habit in aid of bowel movement was smoking. At one time he had a pipe and, in memory of less inhibited Edwardian days, made good use of a spittoon. (After his retirement he discarded both pipe and spittoon and took to cigarettes. At the age of ninety-two he was a twenty-a-day man.) Immediately after breakfast he sat down purposefully by the dining-room fire, lit up and, brooking no interruption, kept on smoking and spitting until the call came.

On weekdays, though sometimes fraught, the operation was fairly leisurely. On a Sunday, because of the half-past-eleven deadline, it was much more furious and concentrated. But when my mother's prayers were answered and the bowel movement was at last successfully accomplished, he would come downstairs, slip-slopping in his slippers. 'Maimie,' he'd shout, 'bring me my boots!' (He never wore shoes, his idea being that they allowed his ankles to get cold.)

The boots would be toasting by the kitchen fire. Maimie would bring them and silently hand them over to my mother in the dining-room. She, devoted soul, would kneel down and patiently help the champ to pull them on and lace them up. Frequently, if she fumbled or her hands got in the way of his hard, darting fingers, she was rewarded by agonized groans of reproof and protest.

Then, exhausted by hard work in the bathroom and by much struggling with his boots, the Padre would lean back in his armchair. 'Mamma, my baking soda!' he'd cry.

'Yes, dear. Just a minute. I'll get it from the kitchen.'

'Look at the time! Nearly half past eleven.'

'There's no hurry. The church is only two hundred yards away.'

'I know, I know. But before you've all titivated yourselves . . . Nobody in this house has any idea of time!'

She would bring the baking soda, mixed in a glass of buttermilk. It was supposed to relieve flatulence, but the way he gulped it down usually aggravated the symptoms. 'I'm not feeling well at all,' he would inform her.

'You'll be fine once you get into the pulpit.'

'Easy to say! Go and get your hat on. And where are the boys? *Chiall beannachd mi*, why can't they be ready when they're wanted?'

But we *were* ready: paternal wrath on a Sabbath morning was even more awful than on week-days. We were lined up in the hall wearing our starched Eton collars, serge suits, knitted stockings and scuff-proof boots. So was Maimie, in frilly grey, a fugitive from cold meats already sliced, the potatoes and vegetables left simmering on the kitchen range.

Our parents led the way to the church, the Padre in black trousers, black frock coat and black, flat-topped clerical hat, my mother at times quite dashing, we thought, in a wide hat, white blouse, dark blue jacket and fashionable 'hobble' skirt. Archie and Willie and I came behind with Maimie – down the Manse drive, along the road and across the gravel towards the vestry door. We remained silent except when we met somebody and grave Sunday morning greetings had to be exchanged.

It used to puzzle us why everything was so 'black' and stern, especially when one of the hymns we were going to sing might well be 'Let all with heart and voice before His throne rejoice'. We had a vague apprehension that it had to do with mourning for the death of Christ. But in our simple minds two questions jostled for answers. Why, when we were taught in Sunday School that Christ died to make us happy, should everybody be so gloomy about it? Was it fair to Him?

Underneath the discipline we were reasonably happy ourselves. We grinned and winked at other boys in similar restraint. Once inside the church and seated in the Manse pew, we settled down contentedly, thinking our own thoughts. These might concern stamps on approval or a big salmon spotted the evening before in the Minister's Lynn or a game of football arranged for after school the following day. They beguiled the long minutes during which we waited with hope for amusing developments during the service.

We enjoyed no deep religious experience; but as we looked round at the congregation, at the sturdy pulpit bulging above the choir stalls, at the two great stained-glass windows on either side of it presented by the Dowager Duchess of Argyll – one in memory of her late husband, the eighth Duke, the other in

memory of Queen Victoria – we had the comfortable feeling
that God was in His heaven and that our world was all right.
The faint odours coming from the water heaters, the paraffin
lamps and the varnished pews, the quietness of the place
suddenly enlivened by the ringing of the old cracked bell (which
had been taken from a ship wrecked on the island of Sanda) –
all added to our sense of security.

Then the bell stopped ringing, Mary Barbour began playing
the organ, pedalling vigorously, and Old Archie the beadle
stumped in with 'the Books' and placed them with professional
reverence in the pulpit. Immediately afterwards the champ made
his entrance, swishing down the aisle resplendent in white
collar bands, black cassock, black robes and the purple hood
of an arts graduate of Glasgow University. My mother, having
assisted Old Archie in the proper dressing of her nerve-racked
husband, slipped into the pew beside us with a shaky smile of relief.

The organ stopped. The Padre stood up in the pulpit, looked
round at the congregation, raised his eyes to the dark pine
beams supporting the roof and, in a loud, authoritative voice,
announced: 'Let us worship God . . .' No sign of frustration or
anxiety marred his holy countenance. After the service visitors
to the church came to my mother and told her of the inspiration
they had received from the calm dignity of his bearing, from the
sincerity of his preaching (which often dealt with the patient
acceptance of suffering) and from the compassionate regard for
humanity evident in all his prayers. My mother would nod and
smile, giving the impression that she was well aware of her
privileged position as helpmeet to such a great and noble
character.

The Padre was a good minister. He was also a good man. But
as far as we were concerned the dog-collar that he invariably
wore never camouflaged his human weaknesses. Many people
in Southend recognized them, too; but I believe his influence in
the parish was all the greater because of them.

There were times, during a service, when his native Gaelic
tongue betrayed him.

He could never pronounce 'Egyptian'. It always came out as 'Eepgyptian', and when he began to read a biblical passage on the subject of the Exodus we were filled with happy anticipation.

Another word he mispronounced was 'bowl'. At home he handled it perfectly, as when, for example he referred to the sugar bowl – which was frequently, four spoonfuls of sugar being his normal ration in a cup of tea. But in church, reading a passage containing the same word, he always said 'bowel'. 'Or ever the silver cord be loosed, or the golden *bowel* be broken . . .' Did he consider 'bowel' a properly 'olde worlde' rendering of Holy Writ, or, in view of the alarms on a Sunday morning, was it a Freudian slip?

Another word with which he had difficulty was 'cock'. The Gaelic for a hill is *cnoc*, pronounced (with a nasal intonation) as 'chrock'. I think confusion must have occurred in his mind between 'cock' and *cnoc*, because sometimes the former would emerge in his preaching as 'crock'.

There was one splendid day – splendid, that is, for us boys and for some youthful members of the choir – when he delivered a sermon on St Peter and 'the crowing of the crock – I beg your pardon, the cock'. He repeated the mistake so often that one young bass singer in the choir contracted a wheezing cough which threatened to become infectious. Eventually the Padre was begging nobody's pardon. Above his gold-rimmed, half-moon spectacles he was glowering in terrible anger at the choir.

The crisis passed, however, and all might have been forgotten had it not been for his habit of never leaving well alone. The following Sabbath he announced his text and then, in a hearty voice, began: 'Last Sunday, my friends, I spoke to you of redemption, taking as my starting point the story of St Peter and the crowing of the crock – ' He paused. The congregation took a deep breath and held it. He flushed bright red and glared at the choir. 'The COCK!' he roared, defiantly. The young bass, with a whine of agony, slipped from his seat and hid himself beneath the book-board.

There followed a silence, broken only by sobs in various parts
of the church, none of which had sad tears in them. The champ
removed his spectacles and began using his eyes like those of a
lion-tamer. Soon he regained control. Holiness was restored.
The sermon continued.

But never again did he refer to 'the crowing of the cock' from
St Blaan's pulpit.

Occasionally Archie and Willie and I were diverted by other
happenings.

There was a Sunday when a sparrow appeared in the midst of
the congregation, flying back and forth between two sides of the
gallery with remorseless energy. Everybody did their best to
ignore it – everybody, that is, except old Hugh McEachran, the
Kirk Treasurer, who made two wild attempts to capture it, on
his second try stumbling over the end of a pew and grabbing
Mrs MacAlpine's new hat instead. The Padre stopped preaching, snatched off his spectacles, fixed his friend Hugh with hot
blue eyes and ordered 'Leave the blasted thing alone!'

There was also the Sunday when a mouse caused havoc.

From time immemorial, like many another church in Scotland, St Blaan's has had a mouse. On weekdays our new organ
is wrapped around in plastic because of it. Seldom, however,
does it appear when the church is full of people, preferring to
remain concealed and warm in the boiler-house.

But on this particular Sunday our mouse did appear, scam-
pering purposefully along the central aisle and then turning left
to dart among the choir girls' feet. A commotion began. Quick
movements were punctuated by squeals and giggles. Long
skirts were wrapped tightly around close-locked knees. The
Padre, on the point of announcing a hymn, looked down with
irritation combined with a fair amount of interest. 'What's
going on?' he demanded.

Encouraged, the young bass went into action. 'It's a mouse,
sir. I'll get it!'

Without delay – and obviously not unwillingly – he plunged
down among the distracted legs of the choir girls, emerging a

few moments later with the mouse in one hand. He held it up for inspection.

The Padre raised a pointing hand. 'Take it,' he began, then paused, searching for the right word. 'Take it hence!' he commanded finally, like a prophet.

The young bass obeyed. The mouse was put back in its proper place among the boiler pipes. There was no danger of it dying for its sins – or for the sins of others. Superstition in Scotland decrees that a church mouse is not for killing.

During the whole incident Archie and Willie and I sat silent. Our eyes were downcast but our hearts were happy. That morning, while the Padre laboured in the bathroom, we had taken some cheese from the pantry when Maimie wasn't looking and had scattered crumbs inside the church, sparsely along the central aisle, generously in the choir stalls. We had tried it once or twice before, without success; but now, at last, the ploy had worked.

This is the first time the truth has been told. I apologize to those former choir girls who are still alive and will, I hope, remain my friends.

After the morning service the Padre was a changed man. A burden had been lifted. Life was good. At lunch he was kind and considerate to us all, basking in my mother's warm praise for his sermon. After lunch he retired to his bedroom for what he called 'my snooze', which sometimes lasted until four o'clock.

When we – 'the boys' as he always called us until the day of his death, at which time I, for one, was over sixty – when we grew up and had attained what he considered to be a suitable state of maturity, he would ask for our opinions regarding his preaching.

'Well, Angus, what did you think of my sermon today? Good, wasn't it?'

Such an approach made it hard to be adversely critical. So I never was. Nor, in fact, had I ever much reason to be. The Padre could compose a first-class sermon, packed with knowledge, both worldly and mystical. As a rule it was generously illustrated by suitable stories, most of which he culled from memories of his own younger days in North Uist and from the writings of F. W. Boreham, the Australian minister whose books, countless in number, were best-sellers in the years following the First World War.

One of his illustrative stories has always been a help to me in times of trouble and confusion. It concerns a painting called *Checkmate*. The picture shows two men playing chess, one glum and despondent, the other moving his queen and triumphantly announcing 'Checkmate!' But when it was hung in the Royal Academy, a study of the pieces on the board by a chess master revealed that the man who has apparently lost can still make a move – and win.

Not long ago I wanted to tell this story on a television programme and tried to find a reproduction of the painting. Surprisingly, all my efforts failed. Everybody I asked had heard of the picture, but none had ever seen a copy or knew the name of the artist. If anyone can tell me who painted *Checkmate* and the whereabouts of the original picture, I should be grateful.

While the Padre was enjoying his 'snooze' and my mother and Maimie had a deserved rest after the events of the morning, we – 'the boys' – were free to follow our own devices, always provided that such devices were in keeping with Sabbath decorum.

If the weather was wet or stormy we stayed indoors and read books chosen from the Padre's wide-ranging library. (I remember three which gave me warm pleasure and probably fuelled my ambition to become a story-teller: *Guy Mannering*, *Lorna Doone* and *Kidnapped*. More than fifty years later I have still to find three contemporary novels with better plots.) But if the sun shone we were out and about, perhaps crawling among the whins on the hill behind the Manse looking for birds' nests, perhaps surveying the river where lurked the red-spotted salmon, perhaps clambering and scuffling along the shore on the trail of interesting flotsam, perhaps visiting Hughie Stewart in his usual 'howff' above the jetty at Dunaverty and listening eagerly to his stories of the sea.

One Sunday afternoon we discovered among the pebbles on Macharioch beach a few fragments of an amber-coloured substance, scarred and sea-washed. We brought them to Hughie.

'Bits o' resin,' he told us. 'They've been lyin' there, at Macharioch, since the wreck o' the *Argo* in 1903.'

'Tell us about the *Argo*, Hughie.'

He was happy to oblige. It is one of the stories that has become legendary in Southend. Some years ago I discovered a more detailed and accurate account of it in the records of the Royal National Life-boat Institution.

In the early morning of 27 February 1903 the *Argo* of Fredestrand in Norway, a barque of 585 tons, was making her way into the Irish Sea through the North Channel. Carrying a cargo of resin, she was coming near the end of a long journey from Wilmington, North Carolina, to London. A stiff southeast wind was blowing, and in the cold and the dark Captain Eilefson found his ship being driven ashore on the Arranman's Barrels, a dangerous reef about two miles east of Dunaverty on the Southend coast. Soon after seven o'clock, just as it was getting light, she struck.

At that time the Campbeltown life-boat was the *James Stevens II*. The coxswain was George McEachran – 'a big burly whiskery man', according to Hughie – with over a dozen rescues to his credit. The standard crew of a sailing and rowing life-boat like the *James Stevens II* numbered sixteen, double the complement of a modern boat. But that morning most of the enrolled members were absent at the herring-fishing, and when she was launched at 9.30 a.m. George McEachran had with him no less than ten volunteers out of a total of fourteen men.

By half past nine the wind changed to a whole gale from the west-nor'-west, and the life-boat, under sail, had to contend not only with heavy seas but also with hurricane squalls carrying sleet and rain. At 11.30 a.m., however, she was standing off the Arranman's Barrels, in full view of the wreck.

George McEachran now found himself with a problem experienced by all life-boat coxswains. To reach the *Argo* he had to go straight in against the gale.

Meanwhile, anticipating what might happen, the life-boat secretary at Campbeltown had asked the Clyde Shipping Company's tug, *Flying Dutchman*, to follow the *James Stevens II*. The tug had done so, and what happened then can best be told, I think, in George McEachran's own account in the official return of service filed by the RNLI:

'When we got beyond the Bastard Rocks, the wind was dead ahead so signalled the tug to take the life-boat in tow. We were towed to within half-a-mile of the wreck. Found *Argo* on a reef of rocks, hull almost under water. Her crew of nine men were in the rigging. Just as we got there her masts broke and fell overboard. The *Argo* was now on her beam ends, and the crew got outside of the hull on the port side. She was fast breaking up, seas breaking over her.

'In the life-boat we let go the anchor to windward and veered down to the wreck. Got a line made fast and hauled alongside after some bother. Got all nine men off (one man helpless through cold, etc.) and immediately picked up anchor and set sail.

'Off Ruadh Point we went alongside the tug and placed the rescued men aboard her for treatment. The tug took the life-boat in tow again and proceeded full speed to Campbeltown, reaching there at 1.45 p.m. The rescued crew were very kindly treated on the tug and supplied with food and warm drinks and dry clothes.

'Shortly after the crew were taken off, the *Argo* broke up or else sank deeper, for only her port rail could be seen above water. Great credit is due to the tug captain for so smartly coming to assist, as otherwise the life-boat might have been too late.

'Before the arrival of the life-boat, three men from the *Argo* had got ashore in the vessel's small boat. Sorry to say, two of these and a landsman had taken a shore-boat to try and rescue the others, but it was blown to sea and no word of her has been got.'

This return of service reveals a life-boat coxswain's typical modesty. George McEachran, who wrote it, remains anonymous throughout, inferring that he acted only as a member of a team, and no doubt this is exactly how he did regard himself. His warm approval of the kindness shown by the tug men to the rescued crew is evidence of a trait in every good coxswain's character – deep concern for the welfare of others. But Hughie Stewart's account was full of praise for the 'whiskery man's' seamanship and for the courage with which he tackled a difficult operation.

Hughie was also able to supply us with two additional pieces of information – one sad, one happy.

The 'landsman' who had tried to row out to the wreck, along with two of the *Argo*'s crew, was a gardener at Macharioch House, in the employ of the Dowager Duchess of Argyll. Weeks later his body and those of the two crewmen were washed ashore on the Ayrshire coast.

The last crewman to be rescued from the barque was, in Hughie's words, 'the cabin boy'. In his arms he carried a fighting black tom cat. He was scratched all over and suffered pain as the salt spray entered his wounds, but 'he hung on like a fury and the cat was saved'.

Hughie had been there that day. He had seen it all happen.

The *Argo* rescue was the first by the Campbeltown life-boat to become internationally famous, and in due course George McEachran and his men were presented with specially minted medals by King Oscar of Norway. I have seen several of these medals, proud possessions in a number of Campbeltown families.

For Hughie the story ended there. For me it didn't.

In the winter of 1951, during a violent storm, the British steamer *Solidarity* was on her beam ends, fifty miles off Romsdal on the Norwegian coast. As her captain said afterwards, 'it looked like curtains' for the twenty-four men on board. Before the radio broke down, however, they had been able to broadcast a distress call, and suddenly, just as they were giving up hope, a small boat appeared, leaping and plunging in the wild sea. She was the Norwegian life-boat *Larvick*. In the next hour, with superb skill, her crew rescued all the British seamen.

In due course the Norwegian life-boatmen received the warm thanks of the British government and were presented with specially minted medals.

When I read this story in the life-boat magazine and remembered Old Hughie's tale of the *Argo* it occurred to me that here was an instance of how the faithful carrying out of an ideal can pay dividends – dividends measured not in cash but in humanity. I suggested to the Padre that he might be able to use it in a sermon. He was immediately enthusiastic and reminded me of another example of the same kind of thing.

A voluntary life-boat service was the brainchild of Sir William Hillary, a sturdy Yorkshireman born in 1771. In the rules of the Royal National Life-boat Institution, founded in 1824, it is laid down that 'the people and vessels of every nation, whether in peace or in war' shall be 'equal objects of the Institution'.

During the Battle of Britain in the Second World War, the life-boatmen of Ramsgate rescued a British airman, whose plane had been shot down in the English Channel. To their astonishment they found he was Pilot Officer Richard Pope Hillary, author of the famous book, *The Last Enemy*. He was also Sir William Hillary's nephew in the fifth generation.

I believe – as my father did – that when properly examined the books of humanity always reveal an impeccable balance.

7

Red Flares on the Iron Rock

Southend is bounded on three of its four sides by the sea. Ever since we were children it has been in the background of our lives, lapping pale blue on summer sand, heaving sullenly against the rocks in a March sou'-easter, raging and bursting high against Dunaverty Rock when a West Indian hurricane trails a dying edge along the Hebrides.

We built Achnamara in 1936, a mile and a half south of the Manse and only a few yards above the beach. On a day of sunlight the reflection of Dunaverty shimmers towards us across Machribeg Bay. When the wind blows, and the North Channel is filled by galloping white horses, spray hurtles like sleet against our front windows, and afterwards, wielding a cleansing hose, Jean is inspired to make a few unladylike comments. During the first week in our new bungalow we went to sleep with the grumble of the waves monotonous in our ears. Since then we have become inured to the sound and are surprised when a visitor remarks on the sea noises outside his bedroom window.

I think that the mood of the sea, as I view it each day from my desk, has an influence on mine and is often the deciding factor in how and what I write. Sometimes it causes a poem to stir inside my head – a poem burgeoning out of formless ancestral memories – and I have difficulty in reminding myself that I do not possess the genius of a poet and that if I want to earn a living I must concentrate on more prosaic and more profitable ways of writing. (But when the urge to poetry is there I believe that my writing, no matter how prosaic the subject, is the better for it: simpler and less involved, because the vision is clearer.)

The sea is like life: you can never be sure of it. There is a Gaelic proverb which says this, and I believe my brothers and I have the same loving, respectful and sometimes vaguely fearful relationship with it as had the Padre and his North Uist forbears.

I think it was from them that Willie inherited his ambition to be a seaman. I remember him at the age of seven climbing a tall copper beech in the Manse garden and sitting there for hours, looking out at Sanda Sound, through which, before Board of Trade regulations were revised after the Second World War, many of the liners bound for America used to pass. The *Caledonia*, pride of the Anchor Line, was one of these. 'Some day,' he would tell us, with confidence, 'I'll be captain of the *Caledonia* and give you all a hoot on the siren when I'm passing.' Twenty-five years later he was – and did.

There was something else we inherited from seafaring ancestors. None of us has ever been troubled by seasickness. During the Second World War Archie and I spent a great deal of time in troopships. Though in the RAF, Kenneth was also faced by long sea journeys, to America for training and to the Far East for operations. During his National Service John sailed to Singapore and back. During *his* National Service, Jock sailed to Cyprus with the Argylls and, on the way home, acted as a ship's policeman. For us all such cruises were happy holidays, our keen appetites assuaged by mounds of tasty rations spurned by less fortunate friends.

Rona had the same immunity.

In the spring of 1947 the three roads to Southend were blocked by heavy falls of snow. Telephone lines were down, drifts piled high above many of the poles; but on the morning of 15 March, for some technical reason, one local subscriber was able to get through to Campbeltown. He reported that our food and fuel supplies were running short and that an expectant mother needed medical aid.

The Campbeltown life-boat was called out, and Coxswain Duncan Newlands made a difficult journey to Dunaverty, carrying groceries, fuel oil, mail and newspapers. He also brought a doctor, a nurse and Rona, who was then a teacher in the grammar school and had been marooned in a Campbeltown hotel for almost a week. As I helped to unload the life-boat Duncan was in one of his puckish, highfalutin' moods. 'I pulled the doctor's leg,' he told me, 'saying it was a pity Rona should be so full of *joie de vivre* while he was so full of *mal de mer*.'

The coasts of Southend are littered with the skeletons of ships. More than 1400 years ago we believe that St Columba, with his discples, made a safe landing from a coracle at Keil. Since then other seamen have not been so lucky. The racing tides at the Mull and the wind swirling and bouncing back off the cliffs at Borgadaile Point, together with the fog which often moves in quietly and quickly across the Firth of Clyde, make navigation in the North Channel difficult even for experts.

On a summer's day the sea around us may look friendly and serene; but because of the sudden changes that can affect our weather any amateur with an urge to sail in it is advised to consult the coastguards before he does so. Every year holiday-makers come with their frail sailing dinghies and fibre-glass punts powered by outboard motors. Every year the Campbel-town life-boat or the local IRB (Inshore Rescue Boat) has to render assistance to somebody whose craft has been overturned by a sudden squall or carried out into dangerous waters by the fast tides. Not long ago one of our girl visitors was rescued by a helicopter. The lilo on which she had been having a restful snooze had drifted out from Dunaverty and was heading rapidly for the Antrim coast.

Centuries ago, when human life was not so tenderly protected as it is in the second half of the twentieth century, gangs of wreckers lured many a vessel to destruction on the black rocks in front of Achnamara. On a dark and stormy night, at a time when Dunaverty Castle was unoccupied by the Clan Donald, they would climb the rock and fix a light on the battlements. Unsuspecting sailors, coming round the Mull, would take it for a light on the island of Sanda and alter course towards what they believed was Sanda Sound but which, in reality, was the jagged shoreline between Borgadaile and Dunaverty. When their vessel struck and they scrambled or swam ashore they would be met by cut-throat ruffians intent upon killing them and looting their cargoes.

Old Hughie Stewart used to tell a story about a Negro slave, the sole survivor from a Portuguese ship wrecked underneath the Borgadaile Cliff. On his back he carried a small wooden barrel containing gold and jewels belonging to his master, the captain. He was able to avoid the wreckers and began climbing the cliff.

This is a difficult and dangerous ploy even in daytime. I remember, several years ago, when a Peterhead fishing-skiff ran aground at the same place, being one of a rescue-party which, as the tide rose, was forced to use the cliff as a means of egress from the shore. Scared almost to the point of paralysis, I couldn't help imagining how the Negro must have felt in the gale-filled dark.

According to Old Hughie, however, he reached the top at last and made good his escape. But – and this is the twist to the tale – at some point in his climb he became so exhausted that he had to abandon the heavy barrel. The story goes that he buried it deep in a crevice in the cliff and that as he never returned to Southend after his ordeal, it must still be there, treasure-trove for a lucky finder.

I thought about this, too, on the day I climbed the cliff but had no desire to tarry in order to make a search.

The rocky shores of Sanda Island, which is part of the parish, are strewn with rotting wood and pieces of rusty metal from the carcases of dead ships. To the north-east of Sanda there is Paterson's Rock, a sharp-toothed islet reckoned to be the deadliest danger to shipping in the whole of the Firth of Clyde. About seventy years ago a diver named Gush was sent down to investigate a casualty on Paterson's Rock. He came up, weeping and on the point of collapse. 'The things I saw! The skeletons and the dead men waving their arms! The fish and the eels, huge and bloated, feeding on the corpses!' He gave up his job and never dived again.

When our visitor friends congregate at the inn to meet us and listen to our local yarns, that one frequently stops the show. There is a more pleasant story, however, about the ship whose long, curved keel and rib-cage can still be seen at low water on Brunerican sands, east of Dunaverty. She was the *Tantivy*, bound for the Clyde with a cargo of oranges from Spain.

It was a spring morning towards the end of last century, and Jean's father, at the time 'a big laddie' according to himself, was working in a field above the shore. Suddenly he saw the *Tantivy*, sails flapping, emerging from the fog in Sanda Sound and heading straight for the sands. He rushed to tell his father, Archie McKerral, who happened to be the Receiver of Wreck, and before the vessel struck almost all the able-bodied men in the parish had gathered and were waiting to give what help they could.

As the weather, apart from the fog, was mild and almost windless, the crewmen were rescued without much difficulty. But almost at once, owing to the ground swell, the *Tantivy* began breaking up. Oranges in their thousands floated ashore. The real job was put in hand, that of salvaging the cargo.

Over the next few days the oranges were taken away in horse-drawn carts and deposited in great yellow pyramids outside Brunerican Farm, under the eye of its tenant, the Receiver of Wreck. People from every part of Kintyre came to see the remarkable sight, some doubtless with the notion that they might be able to 'liberate' the odd orange or two. But Archie McKerral had mounted a strict guard, and soon feelings of frustration occurred, especially amongst the village boys. This, however, was temporarily relieved by the arrival on the scene of a black-bearded foreigner with a barrel-organ and a dancing bear. This man, it appears, was well known throughout Scotland at the period, attending fairs and other gatherings of country folk.

But on the night before the oranges were due to be removed by their owners, the village boys made a final effort. To their

delight they were able to infiltrate the guards and get away with
a whole sackful of fruit. In a dark house in Teapot Lane they
gathered for the feast. Oranges were peeled. Strong white
teeth sank into them. Juice squirted, appetizingly. But then the
groans and the disillusion came. The oranges were for marmalade, so sour as to be inedible.

One of my father's predecessors, the Rev. Peter Thomson,
whose congregation had suffered depletion on account of the
dancing bear, preached a resounding sermon on the subject,
drawing morals by the score. It is said, however, that during the
following week he accepted gratefully the gift of a pot of
marmalade from the mother of one of the boys.

In more modern times, thanks to powerful engines, a watchful
coastguard service, radar and the radio-telephone, wrecks are
not so common on our coasts. But gales still blow and the sea
remains treacherous. In the January tempest of 1953 the
Princess Victoria sank in the Irish Sea with the loss of 133 lives.
Posted at Lloyd's as 'missing' were seven other vessels – the
Swedish steamer *Aspo*, loaded with pit-props, the *Leopold Nera*
from Zeebrugge, the *Salland* taking china-clay to Delfzyl and
four trawlers from Grimsby, Lowestoft and Fleetwood. Power-
driven, and with every available navigational aid at their
disposal, they were all destroyed by the cruel sea. Life-boats
and the devoted men who crew them are still an urgent necessity.

In Southend and Kintyre generally many of our sea stories
concern rescues by the Campbeltown life-boat. One of the most
dramatic occurred when censorship was in operation during the
Second World War and it received scarcely any publicity. I
think this ought to be remedied.

When my old friend Duncan Newlands retired in 1962 he had
been a member of the crew of the Campbeltown life-boat for
forty-one years and coxswain for eighteen. He had taken part
in 100 services and helped to save more than 300 lives.

His decisions were always sharp. When still an ordinary life-
boatman he saw a lug-sail boat capsizing in Campbeltown

harbour and throwing its crew of two small boys into the water. He collected some of his mates at the quay-head, raced for the life-boat – which was lying handy at the pier – got the mechanic to start the motors and took command. Within minutes the boys were rescued and the life-boat was back at her moorings. Only then did Duncan realize the seriousness of his offence. He had, in effect, 'stolen' the life-boat.

Soon afterwards an inspector from the RNLI visited the town, and Duncan was worried: 'I was in a blue funk in case I'd be sacked from the service.' But the local life-boat secretary gave evidence that on the day in question no other boat had been available and that if young Newlands had not acted so promptly the boys would almost certainly have been drowned. After delivering a homily on the rules and regulations of the life-boat service, the inspector smiled, shook Duncan's hand and informed him that he had been promoted to the post of bowman.

Duncan always maintained hard discipline in the life-boat, but his brilliant seamanship and his ability to turn a dangerous situation into a kind of joke gave his crew unquestioning confidence in his leadership. For his part, he has never accepted personal credit for a daring rescue. 'The strength of the coxswain lies in the strength of the crew,' he keeps telling me. 'This is no false modesty. In the life-boat you're neither modest nor immodest: you face facts. Life-boatmen don't go for glory but to help people in distress. Sometimes we actually know the men we are trying to save; and we all have the thought at the back of our minds that it may be our turn next to pray for the help of the life-boat.'

His experience of the coastal waters of the Firth of Clyde has probably never been equalled, and I believe that the contours of the seabed in this area are as clear in his eye as the land-levels are in mine. On the night of 29 January 1945 it was fortunate that he possessed such expert knowledge.

All that day a blizzard had been howling through the streets at Campbeltown. The thermometer at naval headquarters in

the requisitioned grammar school, HMS *Nimrod*, was register-
ing a few degrees below freezing-point. A number of overhead
lines had been damaged by the southerly gale; but the telephone
in the life-boat secretary's home remained in working order. At
6.55 p.m. it began to ring.

The call was from the signal officer in *Nimrod*, relaying the
information that red distress flares had been seen off the south
end of Arran.

Earlier in the day, on account of the deteriorating weather,
the naval authorities had closed the harbour. Shipping was at a
standstill. Because of this A. P. (Tony) MacGrory, the honorary
secretary, had now to go on foot to naval headquarters, so as
to make it clear that the order could not – and would not –
apply to the life-boat. After a considerable argument Tony
MacGrory got his way and with the help of a messenger began
calling out the life-boatmen, running from door to door in the
black-out.

Coxswain Newlands was the first to be told. As he raced down
to the life-boat shed on the New Quay the night was as black as
a peat-bog, with the wind gusting up to force 8. Sea spray
showered across tarred planking and empty bollards. In the
jabbling water under the lee of the pier lay the *City of Glasgow*,
a fifty-two-foot Barnett, moored close to a flight of wooden steps.

Five more members of the crew assembled in the shed – John
McIntyre, second coxswain; Duncan Black, bowman; Duncan
MacCallum, mechanic; and deck-hands James Lang and
Archie Mackay. But two of the regular crew were missing. One,
it appeared, was away from home. Another had a sprained
ankle.

But now a volunteer came forward, offering to fill a place. He
was young Dan Black, a son of the bowman.

Dan was only seventeen and had never been in the life-boat
before, and at first Duncan did his best to dissuade him. But
Dan's father said: 'If he wants to be a life-boatman, now's his
chance to see what it's like.' In the end Duncan agreed to let
him come, because, as he explained afterwards, the Blacks of

Campbeltown had the sea in their blood and service with the life-boat was a family tradition.

As the crew put on their oilskins, sea-boots and life-jackets and listened to the drone outside of the life-boat's motors warming up, Tony MacGrory told them briefly what he knew about the casualty. She was a naval trawler, the *Dunraven Castle*, with a complement of twenty-five officers and men.

Years later I heard the story of the service from Duncan himself. Here it is, with a few salty epithets omitted, but otherwise almost exactly as he told it to me.

'We got into the boat and set off about ten to eight. As the flares had been seen at the south end of Arran, I was pretty sure the wreck would be near the Iron Rock Ledges, so I set a course for them.

'It was wild out there in Kilbrannan Sound. Between the darkness and the clouds of spray – and the snow which stung our eyes like needles – we couldn't see much; but I calculated how long the *City of Glasgow* ought to take for the crossing – just over the hour – and let her go.

'I noticed Dan was a bit shaky. I knew he was thinking about his mother. She'd been through this kind of thing before, first with her own father, then with her husband. However, I reckoned Dan would be all right with the other lads. They'd steady him, and once we got to the wreck he wouldn't have much time to think about anything but the job.

'At nine o'clock I told Duncan MacCallum to slow the engines. Mac and I were in the boat together for a long time and worked very close. I couldn't see a thing but had a notion we weren't far from the Iron Rock Ledges. The lads used to say I smelt my way along, but the answer to that is just experience. Anyway, I told John McIntyre to put up a flare, and there we saw her, three hundred yards away on our starboard bow – the *Dunraven Castle*, fast on the ledges and listing over at forty-five degrees. Almost at once she put up a flare in answer to ours.

'It looked pretty desperate. Between us and the trawler was a scummy mass of foam, heaving about and looking like blood in the light of the flares. Through the snow and the spindrift we could see waves crashing up against her bows.

'I heard Dan saying he was scared. He wasn't the only one. As the life-boat rolled and dived, and the spray lashed into our faces, I kept wondering how the hell I was going to get close enough to do any good. But I said to myself: "Newlands, you're lucky finding her so quick. Keep the luck going, think fast."

'The obvious way in was straight ahead, through a gap in the rocks, but I had a queer feeling. Something kept telling me: "Not that way – watch your step." I'm not superstitious or anything like that. Maybe it was just instinct.

'I could see the lads were wondering what had come over me, so I made up my mind. "We'll go round and approach from the nor'ard," I said. "Then get under her lee."

'John McIntyre thought I was daft. "There's only a couple o' fathoms in the passage there. It's a risk."

' "That's what we're here for," I told him. "To take a risk. Anyway, her bottom's built to take a dunting."

'Dan didn't say anything. He was whiter than a sail, and his face was all eyes. I tried shouting a joke at him, and he did his best to smile back. Then I told Mac to give us three-quarter speed and steered for the passage.

'We went by the casualty broadside, plunging and swinging, with the spray blinding us, and got round on her lee side. We turned and got ready to go in. It was a chancy business, there's no denying it. I knew that with only a couple of fathoms below us the boat might be damaged, but I kept reminding myself that on account of her aircases and watertight compartments she'd still float us home.

'I put her at it, and in the heavy seas we went through that passage like a bucket in a burn. The hull jarred and crunched and bounced, but luckily the rocks were smooth, so we were all right.

'Then we ran into deeper water, swung in towards the *Dunraven Castle* and drove alongside. It would have been dangerous to hit her side on, so I went straight ahead, bow first. We got a bit of a bash as we struck her, but the only damage was to a fender-strap.

'I started using the loud hailer, shouting to the men aboard to catch a line. Duncan fired it, but the trawler's crew didn't seem to hear, and the rope slithered back over the side.

'Having lost way, the life-boat fell off again, so I went astern – and quick at that.

'I kept shouting, trying to tell the navymen that we intended to have another go but that if we didn't make it this time we'd have to lie off until daylight and then their chances would be poor. Whether they heard me or not I couldn't be certain.

'John McIntyre put up another flare and we drove in again. We struck the trawler's side, this time damaging the anchor-stanchion.

'Duncan Black fired a second line, and this time the men aboard must have heard me shouting, because to my relief half a dozen of them showed up at the rail. They caught the line, hauled the wire aboard and made fast.

'I shouted to them to use the wire and come down into the life-boat hand over hand, but at first they wouldn't risk it.

'Then I told John McIntyre to get a preventer out. This is a safety-device – a kind of insurance if you like – a second wire in case the first one bursts. It was a necessity that night on account of the heaving and pounding.

'When John had fixed it, two of the survivors took a chance and swung down aboard us. Just then the main wire burst, but the preventer held the life-boat till we managed to rig a double wire. Then the men began swinging and tumbling down. They were wet and freezing cold and their hands got cut on the wire.

'During one of the poundings, as a solid sea came up and struck our faces and we swallowed pints of salt water, John shouted: "Another one like that and we'll have no boat to take us home!"

' "Don't worry," I shouted back, "I'm just as anxious to get home as you are! I forgot to get insured!"

'Soon all the navymen were in the life-boat except the captain. He was having a last look round his ship, maybe sick in his heart at leaving her. But this wasn't a time for sentiment, because the life-boat was in a tight spot, so I yelled to him to hurry up, and my language wasn't too polite. He came to the rail, then hesitated, looking back over his shoulder. As he stood there another wire burst and he pulled himself together and came scrambling down.

'They were all aboard now, all twenty-five of them. I had a look at my watch and saw that the whole operation had lasted only fifteen minutes. I told Mac to hammer her astern.

'We cleared the rocks, and I set a course for Davaar Island at the mouth of Campbeltown Loch. Mac radioed the completion of the service.

'If anything, the weather was now worse, dark and squally and the snow thicker than ever. All I could see as we made our way across Kilbrannan Sound was the reflection of our green and red navigation lights swinging about on the broken water. It was so cold that I ordered a rum ration to be handed round and had a good swig of ginger-wine myself – being a teetotaller.

'Dan was more settled. He'd gone through a rough baptism all right, but from that time he never looked back. He became a regular member of the crew and one of the best men in the boat, a credit to a great seafaring family.

'We reached the pier at five past eleven and put the survivors ashore. As well as being the life-boat secretary, Tony Mac-Grory was the local representative of the Shipwrecked Fishermen and Mariners' Royal Benevolent Society. He had organized hot drinks, food and dry clothes, helped as usual by the ladies of the Life-boat Guild, and these were now given to the navymen in the life-boat shed.

'I remember that by then the snow had turned to pelting rain.'

When a life-boatman is persuaded to tell a story nobody can tell one better; but he always tends to make it sound far too simple and straightforward as far as his own involvement is concerned. The fact that the *City of Glasgow* went out that night in defiance of the naval authorities, who judged the weather to be too rough even for a life-boat, is mentioned by Duncan only in passing. The seamanship of the crew and his own superb skill – the result of years of experience and intelligent study – are not mentioned. He describes vividly the wild confusion of the sea on the Iron Rock Ledges; but his almost incredible feat of guiding the life-boat through those deadly rocks, in the roaring, spray-filled dark and with the boat swinging and heaving like a maddened animal, is left to the listener's imagination. And when I suggested the word bravery to him in connection with the service, I got an answer: 'Brave – me! You should see me at the dentist's!'

About twenty-five years ago I was writing a series of radio scripts for Kathleen Garscadden of Scottish Children's Hour, the general title being *I'm Proud of My Father*. In each one a child told the story of his or her father, who was, as a rule, a Scotsman of courage. We found firemen, air-line pilots, miners, members of mountain-rescue teams, all of whom were willing to take part. Then I decided that a life-boatman would be an ideal choice for the first programme, and the obvious subject was Duncan.

He is a widower. At the time his only daughter May was in the grammar school, an exceptionally bright pupil keen on the adventure of broadcasting; but she and I faced an almost insuperable difficulty when we tried to sell him the idea of the programme. The prospect of a journey to Glasgow and a long recording session at the BBC filled him with dismay. 'I'm a sailor,' he growled at me, 'no' a bloody play-actor!'

I pointed out that he was showing a selfish spirit: May would be bitterly disappointed if he didn't go, and the RNLI would lose a valuable piece of publicity. As I well knew, nobody is more unselfish than Duncan, and my argument shook him. In the end, gloomy and unwilling, but comforted by his daughter's obvious gratitude, he said: 'All right, be damned to you! But I'm no' wearin' a collar an' tie!'

On the day the three of us went in my car to Broadcasting
House in Glasgow he was wearing a collar and tie and a smart
blue suit: May inherits not only her father's courage but also
her late mother's powerful will. Kathleen Garscadden was
waiting for us. Her crisp friendliness and the fact that her
father had been a sea-captain immediately appealed to Duncan,
and from the beginning they got on famously together. May
and I raised eyebrows to each other in relief.

But when the time came for him to start recording in the
studio there was more trouble. The man who had 'stolen' a
life-boat, who had faced the red turmoil of the Iron Rock
Ledges with scarcely a tremor, who had received more than one
decoration for conspicuous gallantry – this same man was
scared stiff of the microphone. Kathleen and May and I
laboured anxiously to make him go on.

Eventually, however, as Kathleen continued to wield her
charm and May and I used bullying tactics, he forgot about his
'nerves'. As often happens in the case of people initially terrified
of broadcasting he began to tell his stories with a modest conviction which is the mark of the real 'personality'. Only one
incident marred the proceedings. At one point, while recording
a thrilling piece of narrative, he shook Broadcasting House to
the core by stopping abruptly, snatching off his spectacles and
roaring into the microphone: 'Ach, tae hell, ma glesses is a'
steamed up!'

'Oh, Mr Newlands!' exclaimed Kathleen from the production
panel. Dumbfounded engineers pressed buttons. Tapes were
hurriedly rewound and readjusted. May cried, 'Daddy, how
could you!'

Then Kathleen began to laugh. Everybody laughed, including
Duncan. The session continued, the result being a notable
programme still remembered by many children who are now
parents – and even grandparents – themselves.

On the long way home to Kintyre that night we ran into a
blizzard in Glen Croe, north of Inverary. My windscreen wipers
laboured. I dipped the headlights and my eyes found some relief

from a dazzle of driving snow; but even so I had difficulty in seeing the road ahead.

Beside me Duncan said: 'Angus, heave-to!'

'Duncan,' I said, 'in the life-boat you're the coxswain – what you say goes. In the car I'm in command. Right?'

'Oh, sure, sure.'

'We're not going to heave-to. You didn't heave-to on the night you rescued the men from the *Dunraven Castle*.'

'Quite right, Angus. You've got to make up your mind. But I wasn't half as scared that night as I am this minute.'

'The trouble with you, Duncan, is that you're a back-seat driver. You've got to trust your coxswain, in a life-boat or in a car.'

'Man, Angus, you'd make a grand minister! You can argue black is white.'

By the time we got to Inverary the blizzard had thinned out. The rest of the journey to Campbeltown was uneventful as far as driving the car was concerned, and Duncan's conversation made it seem all too short. I remember in particular a story he told me that night about the *Alcyone Fortune*.

In 1947 I wrote my first Children's Hour serial for the BBC. It was called *The Crocodile Men* and both Kathleen Garscadden and I were delighted when it was broadcast – and repeated twice – through all the regions. The following year 'the book of the play' was published.

The opening instalment dealt with a shipwreck at the Mull of Kintyre and with the rescue from the sea of a young native of Madagascar called Trabonjy. After the broadcast one critic said it was most unlikely that an Arab boy would be shipwrecked in the Highlands of Scotland. But on Christmas Eve 1948 the Campbeltown life-boat was called out to the rescue of a British cargo ship, the *Alcyone Fortune*, which had gone aground on Sheep Island, near Sanda. And among the survivors rescued by Coxswain Newlands and his crew was an Arab boy of thirteen, a stowaway from Aden. A great little chap he was, according to Duncan, brave and full of fun. His big brown eyes shone like stars when he saw his first Christmas tree in the foyer of a Campbeltown hotel.

One side of the life-boat picture often left in shadow is the strain imposed on a life-boatman's family when the maroons go off and the service gets under way. But in the radio programme about her father May Newlands, though then only a school-girl, shone a clear light upon it.

'When a gale blows up and Daddy and I are sitting by the fire after supper, I keep looking at the telephone, praying it won't ring.

'Then sometimes it does.

'As long as Daddy has plenty of cigarettes he doesn't worry much. He stuffs them in his pocket, then he's off down the street, running for the life-boat shed. I always want to go with him, to see what's happening; but of course he wouldn't like any fuss like that, so I just have to stay at home and imagine everything.

'I stoke up the fire and make a cup of tea. In about fifteen minutes, when I know the life-boat will be near the mouth of the harbour, I switch on the radio and set it on the trawler-band. Daddy says I should go to bed and sleep, but that would be impossible.

'After a while it begins: "Hullo, coastguard. Life-boat calling. Are you receiving me? Over." Then: "Hullo, life-boat. Coast-guard answering. Receiving you loud and clear. Over."

'From there it goes on – the guiding voice of the coastguard and the answers from the life-boat as Daddy and his men grope for the casualty and eventually find it.

'During the actual rescue there's no transmission, no sound on the trawler-band except an occasional crackle. I sit thinking of them all out there and wishing I could do something about it. But there's nothing I can do except wait. For an hour, two hours, three hours or maybe more.

'The time goes on, and the gale whistles in the chimneys and across the house-tops and I imagine what the sea is like outside the harbour. I try to read, to swot up some history, but it's not easy. I keep telling myself that everything will be all right. It's bound to be all right, because Daddy knows his job and the crew all know theirs. They've been out on stormier nights. Remember the *Dunraven Castle*: that was the worst night of all. But they still came back, and not a single life was lost.

'There's nothing on the radio yet – not even a whisper – and it seems years since it closed down. The telephone rings when you don't want it, but the radio stays silent.

'Then suddenly there are voices, and I forget to be afraid. I seem to listen with every part of me until at last it comes through.

' "Life-boat calling coastguard. Service completed. We've taken off all survivors. No casualty or damage in life-boat. Returning to station now. Over."

' "Coastguard calling. Message received and understood. Well done, lads. Over and out."

'For the first time I feel tired, but I stoke up the fire again and put the kettle on for Daddy's hot-water bottle. I want to go down to the shed to see them coming in, but he doesn't like me to be there. I don't even need to make him a cup of tea, because the secretary and the ladies' Life-boat Guild will have a meal ready for the survivors and the crew.

'I just go on waiting, and at last Daddy comes in and takes off his sea-boots and says it wasn't too bad out there, and I tell him I wasn't a bit anxious.

'And the next day he'll be at his job and I'll be at school, both of us very tired but trying to act as if nothing had happened.'

Why do men like Duncan Newlands, pressed for time and money in the hard business of earning a living, volunteer to join the life-boat, in which they know they will face danger and discomfort for a financial return averaging about 50p per hour? Why do their families put up with it?

Duncan says: 'I get a kick out of helping other folk.'

May is now married, with a daughter of her own. She agrees with her father.

8

Ghoulies and Ghosties
and Long-Leggety Beasties

We were brought up in the Manse as orthodox Christians. Nevertheless, our Celtic ancestry caused us all to retain certain pagan characteristics, mainly in the form of an unwilling belief in superstitions of all kinds.

When Archie played football for Glasgow University, earning a 'blue' on the way, he carried with him a rabbit's foot for luck.

Willie's superstition might better be described as a neurosis. Before eating anything – even a chocolate biscuit stolen from the silver barrel on the dining-room sideboard – he would carefully wash his hands, in case, as he explained, he might be poisoned. An excellent habit no doubt, in moderation, but in his case carried to such lengths that the skin on his hands sometimes became inflamed. I think he forgot his 'superstition' when he joined the merchant navy.

Rona had a special locket which she wore when taking part in competitions at the Gaelic Mod. When she sang solo her handkerchief always had a knot in it.

Kenneth and John declare that with their high academic standards they are above such weaknesses; but I have noticed that when it comes to worshipping certain football teams their high academic standards are inclined to approach remarkably human levels.

Kenneth is an ecumenical miracle, a Presbyterian minister who is also a fervid supporter of Celtic. He has been known to pass himself off as a Roman Catholic priest when attending a match at Parkhead and to keep the crowd around him in happy mood by yelling encouragement to his heroes on the field.

John has been a follower of Clyde since he was a small boy. Well I remember him with tears streaming down his cheeks and with his forehead pressed in anguish against the glass of the dining-room window as the almost inevitable defeat of his team was announced on the radio on a Saturday night. I was with him once at Shawfield when Clyde suffered a one goal defeat owing to a doubtful penalty decision against them. At the end the crowd in the stand rose as one man to boo the referee off the field, and there John was among it, a distinguished doctor and professor of midwifery, highly respected by patients and colleagues alike for his calm, commanding skill: there he was, his stout face purple with anger, his voice high above all others in the vigour of his condemnation. I moved away slightly, pretending not to know him, though in fact I was filled with fraternal admiration.

For myself, I am riddled with superstition. On the way to see an editor or to do a programme with the BBC or STV I would never risk walking underneath a ladder. Every morning for as long as I can remember I have put on my left sock first and my left shoe first. If I reversed the process I suspect that the whole rhythm of my day would be upset.

I recognize the source of this left to right fixation. It came from the Druids, who, when performing religious ceremonies, always marched around their stone cairns from left to right. This, they believed, was the only way they could secure the good will of the sun-god, who moved in the same direction. To march around a cairn from right to left ('widdershins' they called it) would, they believed, summon up the devil. According to the *Glasgow Herald*, this is how they do it in their witches' covens in Bearsden and other unlikely parts of Scotland.

Maimie was, perhaps, the most truly superstitious in our household. Born in Perthshire, the reputed heartland of the small dark men called Picts – later translated into pixies – she gathered supernatural lore about her as a warm and kindly granny gathers comforting shawls. On a midsummer night she saw ghosts on the Manse lawn and met them on the dark winter

road when she went to post letters in the box at the Mill Road
end. The strange thing was that she had no fear of the ghosts she
saw. Her voice would be steady as she told us: 'I met him at the
church corner. Huge and black he was, and his footsteps on
the road made no noise. I just kept on walking with my nose in
the air and pretended not to see him.' She would do just that,
I have no doubt: her small, five foot nothing figure was always
taut with steely courage.

When we asked her why the cuckoo should be called in Gaelic
'the lady of tears', she had a ready answer. 'Don't you know that
the cuckoo was once a beautiful girl who wept so much over her
sweetheart's death that in the end she was changed into a bird?'

'Who by?' inquired Archie.

'Nature,' replied Maimie, firmly and finally.

As children we were taught that Easter is a Christian festival
to commemorate the death and resurrection of Christ. Only
later did we realize that in fact it is a Christian graft upon pagan
spring rites dating back into prehistory. We had no idea that
our painted Easter eggs and the Good Friday pancakes baked
by Maimie in a hot confusion of eggs, flour, milk, girdles and a
roaring fire in the kitchen range were symbols of new spring
life in ancient Egypt, Greece and Rome long before Christ was
born. Nor did we know that the Jews still include eggs in their
Passover feast in celebration of their breaking out of slavery in
Egypt, as the chicken breaks out of the egg. We enjoyed eating
the hard-boiled eggs and Maimie's sugared pancakes – that was
all that mattered. And to anyone who believes in Christ, isn't it
all that should matter? Christianity developed out of paganism,
and Christianity teaches that all humanity is one.

The Padre, often accused by the Rev. Kenneth MacLeod
and my mother of being partly a superstitious pagan, denied the
charge only with meagre conviction. His memory was full of
superstitions taken from North Uist, which, when the mood
took him, he would recount to our delight. I am certain that
despite genuine religious rectitude he believed in them.

The story which appealed most to my romantic spirit concerned a Spanish lady seen by a grand-uncle of his on the *machair* near Claddach Kirkibost.

He and his girl were snuggled among the bent, in the gloaming of a summer day. The light on the sea and in the sky was luminous, causing the land to appear shadowed. A movement among the dunes attracted their attention. They sat up, startled, and saw a lady in a Spanish costume gliding past, only a few yards away. There was no sound, except that of the sea caressing the shore. They held each other close, for comfort. Then the girl caught her breath as the Spanish lady stopped and held out her arms and the shadow of a man came towards her. The Padre's grand-uncle used to tell his friends that at this moment the hair at the back of his neck began to prickle. He had a premonition that something terrible was going to happen. But nothing did, except that before the Spanish lady and the ghostly man could meet they both suddenly vanished.

'My grand-uncle and his girl were not the only people who saw the Spanish lady,' my father would tell us, a youthfully gaping audience. 'Many a time, as darkness came over the land and the sky remained bright, she was seen flitting among the dunes, as if lost and looking for someone. When I grew up I made inquiries and discovered that in the seventeenth century a MacDonald, one of the Lords of the Isles, married a Spanish lady and brought her to live in North Uist. Apparently it was an unhappy marriage, because of MacDonald's rough behaviour and his long absences fighting for his clan, and the Spanish lady fell in love with the young son of a local landowner. His name was MacRurie, and in fact he was related to the MacVicars. (According to the Padre, nearly everybody who ever lived in North Uist was related to the MacVicars, and perhaps he wasn't so far wrong at that.) One version of the story – the official MacDonald version – is that the lady and MacRurie fled together from the island and went to live in Spain. Another, secretly whispered, is that MacDonald came home unexpectedly, found his wife and MacRurie together on the machair and killed them both.'

At this point my father would pause, look intensely serious
and say: 'I am sure that if you dug among those dunes you
would find their bones, deep down.'

When Willie and Kenneth and I returned home after the
Second World War he told us that every time we had been in
grave danger he had known of it. This was because of a recurring dream – the dream of a ship on a stormy sea, with one of
us standing in the bow. It had come to him first when Willie
went missing after the sinking of the *Britannia*, and he had been
comforted when the dream ship had not gone down. The next
time was after the landings in Sicily, in which Archie with the
Argylls and I with the RSF were later involved. My ship had
not gone down, but Archie's had, and a few days later news of
his death reached the Manse. Again, while Kenneth was
missing in Burma, the dream had recurred several times; but
the ship with Kenneth in the bow had remained afloat.

He firmly believed in what we call in Scotland 'the second
sight', and many were his tales from North Uist about ghostly
funerals passing a seer's house before they actually took place.
He was confident that my mother possessed it, because she
always seemed able to forecast his behaviour and that of her
sons. She would laugh scornfully at the idea and declare that
she only exercised common sense and a woman's natural
knowledge of her family's characteristics. I must admit, however, that we were all uneasy when we went 'a kennin' wrang',
in case she did have a mysterious ability to find out about it.
Often I saw my guilt reflected in her big green eyes.

There was a legend from her homeland in North Argyll
which she often quoted as proof of her 'practical' turn of mind.

'Between Duror and Kentallen,' she would begin, 'there used
to be a hillock known as *Sithean na Cailliach*, 'the knoll of the
old woman'. Nobody knew the origin of its name, but it was
supposed to be haunted, a place where pixies gathered. Nonsense, of course. I don't believe in hauntings or in pixies. No
true Christian ever does,' she would add, with a sidelong glance
at the Padre.

'When the railway was being built from Ballachulish, *Sithean na Cailliach* was excavated, and inside it was discovered a stone coffin containing bones. Archaeologists said they were those of a woman less than five feet tall, who had probably lived during the Bronze Age. Everything, you see, has a practical explanation if you take the trouble to find it.'

'But what about the ghosts and the pixies?' I asked.

'People never saw them. They imagined them, just as your father and his friends in North Uist imagined things.'

And that was that, except that when the Padre and his cronies would be telling ghost stories late at night she always refused to go to bed before he did.

The Padre often teased my mother by accusing her clan, the MacKenzies, of being on the 'wrong' side at Culloden, that is, against the Jacobites. If she ventured to suggest that the MacVicars hadn't been there at all, on any side, he would remark in a superior way that the MacVicars had been in the navy – supporting the Jacobites, of course. But if he really wanted to annoy her he would attribute what he insisted was her second sight to an ancestral gift handed down by the Brahan Seer, whose name was Kenneth MacKenzie.

'Coinneach Odhar was of a different family of MacKenzies altogether,' she would say, tartly.

'He lived in Ross-shire. So did your forbears, before they fled south to Appin.'

'They didn't flee. They came because they were put out of their crofts.'

'Yes, by the Seaforths, who hated the Brahan Seer and wanted rid of all the MacKenzies.'

'The Seaforths were MacKenzies themselves. Of the same clan as my family.'

At this point the Padre would become jauntily sarcastic. 'Boys,' he'd declaim, 'down on your knees and pay homage to the Countess of Seaforth!'

Kenneth MacKenzie – Coinneach Odhar, or 'dun-coloured

Kenneth' – was the most famous of all Highland seers. His prophecies were written about and authenticated by men of such disparate philosophies as Sir Walter Scott and Sir Humphrey Davy. Among the people of Ross-shire he remains a figure as romantically real as Bonnie Prince Charlie. And yet, strangely, though he is supposed to have lived in the seventeenth century, a well-documented period in Scottish history, there is no contemporary written evidence that he existed.

The Padre had no doubt that he was a real person. My mother suspected that his name was a collective one – like that of some Old Testament prophets – covering the forecasts of many astute and far-seeing Ross-shire men.

According to tradition he was born at Baile-na-Cille in the Ness district of the island of Lewis. It is probable that he was illegitimate, because though his mother figures in many stories there is no mention of his father. As a child he came into possession of a small round stone, coloured blue and with a hole in the middle, which gave him the power of divination. Where the stone came from is as great a mystery as the life of the Brahan Seer himself; but there is a tale that when Coinneach first looked through the hole and found that by this means supernatural powers were conferred upon him, it deprived him of the sight of his right eye and that he continued afterwards to be what is called in Gaelic *cam*, that is, blind of an eye.

Being born on lands belonging to the Seaforths in Lewis, Coinneach Odhar eventually travelled east to work for the third Earl on a farm at Loch Ussie, near the family's seat at Brahan Castle in Ross-shire. There his fame as a prophet quickly spread and he was appointed Seer to the Seaforths. In those days most 'official' seers carefully predicted great triumphs for their clan and confusion for their enemies. Coinneach never stooped to 'popular' forecasts. This was to lead to his tragic end.

A portrait of Isabella, who was Countess of Seaforth at the time, hangs in Fortrose Town Hall. Her husband went to France on business and was a long time coming back. She ordered Coinneach to tell her why. At first he refused to answer, but when she insisted he said: 'At this moment your Lord is on his knees to a French woman. His arms are about her waist and his lips pressed to her hand.'

The Countess was furious. She had Coinneach arrested and tried for witchcraft, and he was condemned to be burned alive in a spiked barrel full of tar. At Chanonry Point near Fortrose there is a memorial stone, erected by the Gaels of Ross-shire, which marks the supposed site of this atrocity.

Before Coinneach died he uttered the best known and most terrible of all his predictions:

'I see into the future, where lies the doom of the House of Seaforth. MacKenzie to MacKenzie, Kintail to Kintail, Seaforth to Seaforth, all will end in extinction and sorrow. I see a chief, the last of his house, and he is both deaf and dumb. He will be father to four fine sons but he will follow them all to the grave. He will live in sorrow and die in mourning, knowing that the honours of his line are extinguished for ever and that no future chief of MacKenzie shall ever again rule in Kintail. Lamenting the last of his sons, he shall sink in sorrow to the tomb and the last of his possessions shall be inherited by a widow from the east who will kill her own sister.

'As a sign that these things are coming to pass there will be four great lairds in the days of the last Seaforth. Gairloch shall be hare-lipped; Chisholm shall be buck-toothed; Grant shall be a stammerer and Raasay an idiot. These four chiefs shall be neighbours and allies of the last Seaforth and when he looks round him and sees them he will know that his sons are doomed to die and that his broad lands shall pass to strangers and his race come to an end.'

There is no possible chance that this prophecy was made after the event, because Sir Walter Scott knew about it – and quoted from it – while the last chief was alive and two of his sons were still in good health.

Francis Humberstone MacKenzie, Lord Seaforth and the last Baron of Kintail, appears to have been a man of character and distinction, 'a nobleman of extraordinary talents', wrote Sir

Walter, 'who must have made for himself a lasting reputation,
had not his political exertions been checked by painful natural
infirmity'. At the age of sixteen he had become stone deaf after
an attack of scarlet fever. He was also afflicted by a serious
speech impediment, which resulted in his having to do most of
his communication in writing. Despite all this, however, he
patronized the liberal arts, encouraged young and struggling
artists like Thomas (later Sir Thomas) Lawrence, was member of
Parliament for Ross-shire for a number of years, raised during
the war with France a regiment of Ross-shire Highlanders (the
78th) and ultimately attained the rank of Lieutenant-General
in the Army. For six years he was Governor of Barbados.

Was he aware, I wonder, as with courage he pursued his
public duties, that his contemporaries, the four lairds of
Gairloch, Chisholm, Grant and Raasay, were all deformed in
the way foreseen by Coinneach Odhar? Old men and women
among his tenantry knew the situation only too well. They
shook their heads, murmured in the Gaelic – and waited.

Lord Seaforth had four sons and six daughters. The eldest
son died in infancy. The second died young; the youngest died
in 1813 and the third and last, 'a young man of talent and
eloquence who represented Ross-shire in Parliament', during
the following year.

In the meantime Lord Seaforth's property in the West Indies
had been so badly mismanaged that straitened financial circumstances compelled him to dispose of part of his Kintail estates,
which included the 'gift land' of his family. His tenants offered
to buy the land for him so that it might not pass from the
MacKenzies, but before this could happen his last son died and
he himself became physically and mentally paralysed. The
tenants bowed to what appeared to be the awful inevitability of
Coinneach Odhar's prophecy. Their offer was withdrawn.

After the death of his last son, Lord Seaforth lingered on, his
fine intellect enfeebled but, according to Sir Walter Scott, 'not
so entirely obscured but that he perceived his deprivation as in
a glass, darkly'. Sometimes he was anxious and fretful because

he did not see his son. Sometimes he complained that his boy
had been allowed to die without his seeing him. But in January
1815 the last of the Seaforths died. And then:

> Of the line of MacKenneth remained not a male
> To bear the proud name of the Chief of Kintail.

But the Brahan Seer's 'revenge' was not yet complete.

On Lord Seaforth's death his Highland estates, with all their
burdens and responsibilities, devolved upon his eldest daughter,
the widow of Admiral Hood. She later married James Stewart
MacKenzie, member of a Galloway family. One day she was
driving her pony-trap, with her sister Caroline as passenger,
when the horse bolted and Caroline was killed.

Thereafter, according to Alexander MacKenzie in his book,
The Prophecies of the Brahan Seer (first published in 1899), 'one
section after another of the estates had to be sold. The remain-
ing portion of Kintail, the sunny braes of Ross, the church
lands of Chanonry, the barony of Pluscarden and the Island
of Lews [Lewis] – a principality in itself – were disposed of,
one after the other'.

Now, finally, the doom of the Seaforths as pronounced by
Coinneach Odhar was fulfilled in every detail.

The story sends a shiver down my spine. Possibly I may and
probably I may not have the blood of Kenneth MacKenzie in
my veins; but if ever I find a blue stone with a hole in it on the
shore near Achnamara I will throw it far out into the sea. It's
one thing to peer through a glass, darkly, as most writers do;
quite another to see face to face.

Many other predictions said to have been made by the Brahan
Seer have come true.

The sulphur and chalybeate spring at Strathpeffer was known
to him, and he foresaw its future. 'Uninviting and disagreeable
as it now is with its thick crusted surface and unpleasant smell,
the day will come when it shall be under lock and key and
crowds of health and pleasure seekers shall be seen thronging

its portals in their eagerness to drink the waters.' The spring
was commercially 'discovered' in the eighteenth century. Later
a pump-house was built and the town advertised as Strathpeffer
Spa, 'the Harrogate of the North'. For many years it did
thriving business.

Nowadays 'taking the waters' at Strathpeffer is not so
popular; but sufferers from rheumatism still drink from the
spring, hoping for relief. I tried it once, and the only liquid I
have ever considered more revolting was a nameless green
liqueur which Jock brought home after a football reporting
trip to Italy. (Jock himself used it as a weedkiller.)

Beyond the towers of the Cathedral of St Andrew in Inverness
there is a small hill called Tomnahurich. It is supposed to mark
the burial place of the Feinn, three giants of ancient Scotland.
A bugle is buried with them, and it was foretold that if the bugle
were blown three times the Feinn would rise and free Scotland
from her oppressors. One day, long ago, a shepherd boy found
an opening in the hill and went inside. He saw the bugle and
blew it, not once but twice. To his horror he saw three huge
figures stirring in the dark and rising on their elbows. He
dropped the bugle and fled, and no one has ever found the
opening again. According to the legend, therefore, the Feinn are
still there, resting on their elbows, waiting for the third bugle
blast to summon them to the aid of their country. (I dedicate
this story to the SNP. Does it not contain some good material
for propaganda?)

With all its ghostly attributes Tomnahurich was a natural
object for the Brahan Seer's interest; and, indeed, he made
two prophecies about it.

The first: 'I see the Fairy Hill under lock and key, with
spirits of the dead secured therein.' In 1846 an area of ground
including Tomnahurich, the Fairy Hill, became a cemetery. It is
surrounded by a fence, with a gate which is locked at night.

The second: 'Strange as it may seem to you, the day will
come when full-rigged ships with sails unfurled will be seen
sailing east and west by the back of Tomnahurich.' This fore-

saw the building of the Caledonian Canal by Telford in 1822. Its exit to the Pentland Firth runs past the Fairy Hill.

A prophecy by the Brahan Seer which appeared to be unlikely at the time it was made: 'A Lochalsh woman shall weep over the grave of a Frenchman at the burying-place of Lochalsh.' Centuries later a wealthy laird of the district engaged a French footman who fell in love with and married a local girl. Soon afterwards the Frenchman died, leaving the widow to mourn over his grave.

'The day will come,' declared Coinneach Odhar on another occasion, 'when two false teachers shall come from across the seas. At that time there will be nine bridges in Inverness. The streets will be full of ministers without grace and women without shame.' Some people claim that in this prophecy the Brahan Seer was referring to the evangelists Moody and Sankey, who, a hundred years ago, wrote 'pop' hymns and made an attempt to revolutionize the sombre religion of the Highlands. But I'm not so sure. The bit about 'ministers without grace' would appear to indicate a more modern trend in clerical attitudes. And could 'women without shame' be an allusion to the mini-skirt? Any day now, I think we ought to be on the look-out for those 'two false teachers'. From America?

That the following prophecy has been fulfilled there can be little doubt: 'The day is coming when there will be a ribbon on every hill and a bridge on every stream. I see a mill on every river and a white house on every hill. Dram-shops will be open at the head of every plough furrow and travelling merchants will be so plentiful that a person can scarcely walk a mile on the road without meeting one. There will be men of law at every street corner.' In Coinneach's day Ross-shire was a wilderness traversed only by footpaths, crude tracks and river fords. Long after his death meal-mills powered by water-wheels became common in the county, and many new shooting-lodges and holiday-makers' houses – most of them white-washed – were built among the rolling hills. Today the area is serviced by ribbons of tarmacadamed roads and modern bridges, used frequently by butchers and bakers and candlestick-makers going their rounds in vans and cars. 'Men of law' stand at street corners in every town, in the shape of burly policemen.

'The day is coming when fire and water will run in streams side by side through the streets of Inverness.' This prediction was proved valid when gas and electricity and a mains water-supply were installed.

'Soldiers will come from Tarradale to the Muir of Ord in fiery chariots without horses or bridle.' Trains, buses and fast cars have made this come true many times.

But now, finally, here is the most fascinating of all the Brahan Seer's prophecies. I give it in composite form, though some of the predictions were made separately, at different times. In it he foresees not only the history of the Highlands and Islands from the Clearances until the present day but also what lies ahead of us.

'The day is coming when the Big Sheep will over-run the Highlands, putting the plough into the rafters and driving cattle into the northern sea. They will become so numerous that the bleating of one shall be heard by another from Lochalsh to Kintail. Clansmen, turning effeminate, will flee the country, seeking comfort in faraway places not yet known. Clansmen who remain will become degenerate, and strange merchants will appropriate the lands of the chiefs. The sheep will be gone, and in their place deer will roam a deserted land. Then will come the time of the Black Rains. They will kill the deer and wither the grasses. After that the people will return and take possession of the land of their ancestors.'

This gives a true picture of what happened in the north and west of Scotland after Culloden. The clan chiefs and the big landowners replaced the old form of agriculture (crofting and cattle-rearing) with a new one involving sheep and shepherds from the Lowlands. Crofters were evicted with a terrible, uncaring cruelty which appears almost incredible to us, reared in a gentler and more humane society.

The best and most readable book on the subject is *The*

Highland Clearances (first published by Secker & Warburg in 1963), a carefully researched and brilliantly written documentary by John Prebble, who, for 'a man of Kent', has a remarkable insight into the Highland character and a deep compassion for the victims of the Clearances. For example, his description of the treatment of the Sollas crofters in North Uist, about which I have written in a previous chapter, carries within it the same ring of authenticity and the same feeling of sad anger evident in the stories handed down by my great-grandfather, a contemporary witness.

As far as Coinneach Odhar's prophecy is concerned, the Seer's reference to 'faraway places yet unknown' is explained by the emigration of the evicted families to America, Canada, Australia and New Zealand. By 'strange merchants' he may have meant the rich industrialists who bought estates from the impoverished chiefs during the nineteenth century and stocked them with grouse and deer for seasonal slaughter.

But what is the significance of the Black Rains? Did Coinneach see the black oil pouring in from the North Sea? Or was he trying to warn us about a nuclear catastrophe and the inevitable fall-out?

Whatever the truth, the prophet of Kintail has bequeathed to me a Hebridean legacy of uneasiness.

In Kintyre, unlike Ross-shire, we have no mysterious figure like the Brahan Seer in the background of our lives. Perhaps the mingling of Lowland elements with native Gaelic blood has caused the Kintyreans to become more hard-headed than our neighbours in the north. There is superstition, but we never take pride in being superstitious.

Beneath a crust of Christian philosophy and secular education, the Padre was highly superstitious, as might be expected in a son of North Uist. But among his parishioners he stoutly denied his birthright and publicly condemned superstition as being anti-religious.

Though accustomed as a boy to the handling of small boats,

he would never, if he could help it, take a sea-trip with Archie Cameron or any of the local fishermen. The old belief that a minister in a boat is unlucky was always at the back of his mind; he was afraid his sea-going friends might resent his company.

As proof of his good judgement in this respect he liked to tell a story about a fellow minister in Campbeltown, who persuaded his leading elder, the Provost of the burgh and owner of two fishing-skiffs, to let him take part in a night's fishing in Kilbrannan Sound. Seine-netters work in pairs. That night, though all the other boats had splendid catches, the Provost's pair, one of which the minister was helping to crew, caught scarcely any fish at all.

In the morning the fleet returned to Campbeltown, the Provost's skiffs, light from lack of herring, reluctantly bringing up the rear. The main body got safely into harbour, but when the laggards were about half a mile from the entrance to Campbeltown Loch, a bank of fog drifted across from Davaar Island. The skippers reduced speed and crawled along; but just before the Provost's skiffs emerged from the fog they collided. Severe damage occurred; and a young fisherman in the boat with the minister aboard had an arm broken.

I can vouch for the truth of this story. It happened while I was editor *cum* reporter *cum* office-boy on the *Campbeltown Courier*, and I printed it. I can also vouch for the fact that as long as he remained in Campbeltown the minister concerned never went herring fishing again.

Once, as Clerk to the Presbytery of Kintyre, my father had to attend an important meeting in Islay. Much against his will, he was persuaded by colleagues to book a seat in the service plane from Campbeltown. It meant that instead of enduring a roundabout journey by bus and steamer via Tarbert, which lasted many hours, he could reach Islay in less than twenty minutes.

'A minister in a plane,' he grumbled to my mother. 'It's unlucky.'

'Oh, nonsense! The Moderator of the Kirk flies everywhere nowadays.'

'The Moderator is different. For a year at least he's not an ordinary minister. As the boys say, he has a "hot-line". Anyway, I don't like flying.'

'How do you know? You've never flown before.'

'That's what I mean. And if God is good to me I'll never fly again.'

The day of the great adventure dawned bright. My mother got up and opened the bedroom curtains. 'Time to get up, dear. It's a beautiful morning. You'll have a perfect flight.'

'All very well for you!' came a voice from the bed. 'If you think it'll be so perfect why don't you go in my place?'

In the car he was silent and on edge, all the way to the airport at Machrihanish. He climbed aboard the seven-seater Rapide with dignified resolution, like Lord Lovat on his walk to the scaffold. The door was closed. Kenneth stood on the tarmac, waiting dutifully to wave farewell.

At first the engines wouldn't start. An agonized face above a dog-collar was pressed to a window. Kenneth made encouraging thumbs-up gestures. Then the face was hurriedly withdrawn as the engines did start. The Rapide taxied to the runway. Kenneth waved as it rose on balanced wings and circled round, heading for Islay. Next minute it was heading back.

It landed and taxied to a stop near the airport office. Two mechanics hurried aboard, and the news circulated that the trouble was superficial: a minor fault in the radio. Passengers were not allowed off.

Again the face appeared at the window, more desperate than ever. Kenneth's heart bled for his father. Somebody beside him said, with a laugh: 'So there's a minister on board. We might have known.'

After a few minutes the Rapide took off again. Kenneth watched until it was a speck in the sky, losing height for Machrie airport in Islay. He was pretty sure of one thing: its clerical passenger would return the next day by way of Tarbert.

He was right. And the Padre never flew again.

A hundred and fifty years ago, in the Highlands and even in Southend, if a farmer's cattle beast took ill, there would be murmurings that 'the evil eye was on it'. An animal so afflicted was often treated by a 'wise woman', who spoke Gaelic incantations over it and then tied a piece of red worsted around its tail as an accessory to healing. Sometimes this custom was used to advantage by 'con men' in the parish.

A story is told about one hard case – his name, it appears, was Hector Mor (Big Hector) – who planned to buy a heifer on the cheap. Before the market opened he picked out the beast he coveted and surreptitiously tied a piece of red worsted around her tail. When the bidding began, other less pragmatic farmers noted the evil sign and averted their eyes. Hector was able to buy her for a song.

In the middle of last century Southend had a 'wise one', who, according to herself, was able to banish the evil eye and effect a cure. Most people were a little afraid of her. Playing on old superstitions, she made a good living for herself.

Jean's great-grandmother, Margaret McKerral, was one of those who took the 'wise one' seriously, though her husband, Old Hugh, would have no truck with such 'pagan nonsense', as he called it. Once, when a cow on Brunerican Farm became sick and refused to give milk, Margaret called in the 'wise one'. This was in direct opposition to Old Hugh's wishes; but Margaret was sure that if she didn't ask for the woman's help the evil eye would kill the cow.

Following the ritual of the 'cure', the wise one placed a ladder against the outside roof of the byre and climbed to the eaves. First she poured water on the thatch – water into which she had dipped some silver coins given to her by Margaret. Then she began pulling at the thatch, as if she were milking a cow, and muttering an incantation: 'Come, my darling! Give good milk to slake the thirst of the Druids!'

Suddenly, in the middle of it all, the ladder slipped. Squealing with alarm, the wise one fell to the ground and injured her leg.

Margaret McKerral was a kindly woman. Her faith in the

wise one was shattered, but she took her into the house and nursed her until her leg was better.

During this time the cow recovered naturally, and Old Hugh – refraining with a struggle from saying 'I told you so' – was able to convince his wife that the wise one had very little wisdom after all and that superstition was bunk.

Some day, perhaps, the pagan fears born within us will be transmuted into something happier – an untroubled sense of wonder.

I used to write science fiction for children, telling stories about lost planets, space life-boats and other objects of my imagination. I think I did it partly as a kind of release from inherited superstition concerning the unknown. Then Neil Armstrong stepped down from his space-ship on to the surface of the moon and I decided, for a time at least, to give it up. Facts had overtaken fiction. Today the achievements and discoveries of real-life scientists are to me far more wonderful than fiction – or superstition – could ever be.

Take an example. Out there in the indigo dark of space are millions and millions of stars: so many millions, indeed, that the scientists, employing statistical methods, have come to the conclusion that somewhere there must exist other worlds like ours, with creatures similar to us living on them. (Creatures who possibly find it as difficult as we do to understand – and to solve – the problems of living.)

Faced by this astonishing idea, I ask the question: 'How was such a vast universe of stars – such an unimaginably vast universe of stars – first created?' Again the scientists provide an answer. Long ago, on the very threshold of time, a gigantic explosion occurred in space, and our whirling, expanding galaxies, receding from one another even yet at a fantastic rate, are the result of it. They call it the 'big bang' theory.

But at this stage it occurs to me to wonder who created the matter that existed *before* the big bang. Neither the scientific nor the superstitious can answer that one.

9

There is Nothing like a Dame

We found it difficult, as children, to decide who was in command – the Padre or my mother. Making loud noises, threatening and dispensing punishment with a hair-brush, issuing orders to my mother and Maimie regarding his meals, his boots and his clothes, from the pulpit uttering the word 'Almighty' with such unction that he appeared to be suggesting a close personal relationship, the Padre presented the image of a man in authority, the veritable captain of his ship. It was only when sealed lofts began to be opened, and we were able to study the situation in greater depth, that we recognized my mother's power and influence in most of the decisions he made.

She handled him like a trainer with a tiger, showing kindness and understanding and a calm disregard of temperamental outbursts, but occasionally using a whip of the tongue when such an approach seemed justified. She never quite tamed him; but on most occasions, if there occurred a clash of wills, it was my mother's which prevailed. It was she who instilled in us 'the fear of the Lord' which is 'the beginning of wisdom', the ambition to make the most of what talents we possessed and the concept that it is self-discipline and not 'doing one's own thing' that leads to the good and happy life.

Her personality was quieter and less dramatic than the Padre's; but in the end we decided that hers was the stronger. Her faith was tempered steel.

Early in life we realized that the same could be said about many of the ladies of Scotland. In those days, when grey lava from the volcano of the industrial revolution was still flowing, farmers and farm-workers, neglected and almost forgotten by governments dedicated to 'big business' and an urban way of life, lived on the edge of poverty. Their womenfolk had no advantages, except those conferred on them by fresh air and an uncomplicated way of life. They worked at the milking, morning and evening, week in week out, and at the back-breaking tasks of making butter and cheese. The 'pill' had not been invented, and they bore large families and knitted and sewed and cooked for them. But all the time they had a deciding voice in the conduct of their men, and as a result the Kirk was well attended and the parish full of good neighbours. I often heard my father say: 'If you ever want anything done in Southend, get the women on your side.'

Today, when they are 'liberated', when agricultural pros-perity has taken the place of penury, when on dairy farms the milking is done mechanically and on beef farms there is no milking at all, when butter and cheese are made at the cream-eries, when families can be planned and there is plenty of money for the purchase of spin-driers, dish-washers, freezers and other labour-saving devices, they occupy a more influential place than ever in the life of the community.

A farmer's wife used to be old, bent and 'done' at sixty, wearing a drab high-necked blouse and a 'druggit' skirt and apron. Now at the same age she looks like a fashion picture in the *Scottish Field*, drives her own car, plays golf and goes swimming whenever the mood takes her. The men 'plough and sow and reap and mow', as a rule sitting on a tractor; they tend the cattle and sheep and go to market. Many of them allow their well-educated wives and daughters to do 'the books' and decide on domestic policy. Any sharp analysis of the situation reveals that the parish is run mainly by the ladies.

All this is probably due to our inheritance from the Celts, who were a matriarchal society. And it is significant that in our Scottish history there seem to be far more notable women than men. Those range from Malcolm Canmore's wife, Queen Margaret, who, in the eleventh century caused many churches and 'welfare houses' to be built thoughout the kingdom, from Mary Queen of Scots, whose royal good sense was betrayed by a human need of love, from Flora MacDonald, the Jacobite heroine, down to our own contemporary, Winnie Ewing, who cocked a snook at the modern Whigs and Tories and gave a refreshingly different slant to the news.

As far back as the thirteenth century, the influence of the ladies was evident in a Scottish Act of Parliament, which ordained that 'ilk maiden ladye of baith highe and lowe estait shall hae libertie to bespeak ye man she likes; albeit, gif he refuses to tak her till be his wyf, he shall be mulcted in ye sume of ane hundredth pundid or less, as his estait may be, except and alwais gif he can mak it appear that he is betrothit to ane ither woman, then he shall be free'.

Most visitors to Scotland throughout the centuries have praised the ladies. Aeneas Sylvius from Italy, who afterwards became Pope Pius II, made a Scottish pilgrimage in the fifteenth century and found them 'good looking and comely', though he does add an embarrassed footnote: 'They are lavish with their kisses, giving their lips as freely as do Italian women their hands.' I suspect that Aeneas was a considerable heart-throb himself.

At about the same time another foreigner came to Scotland. He was Don Pedro de Ayala from the Spanish court of Ferdinand and Isabella. He described the Scottish ladies as being graceful and handsome, exceedingly courteous and honest, though he, too, has a word of criticism for what he calls their 'boldness'. 'They dress much better than the English women,' he goes on, 'are so fond of foreigners that they dispute as to who shall entertain them, and are absolute mistresses of their own homes, and even of their husbands.' (I like his use of the word 'even'.)

Oddly enough, it was English visitors who often seemed to be less than complimentary.

For example, Thomas Kirke, author of a book published in 1679 called *A Modern Account of Scotland by an English*

Gentleman, had nothing good to say about the Scots at all, whatever their sex. According to him they were 'arrogant, vainglorious, bloody, barbarous, inhuman and proud'. The women, he adds, had 'legs like strong-posted timber', a discourteous allusion, I should guess, to the thickness of their ankles. And his most terrible indictment of all: 'They dislike Englishmen!' I have a feeling that somehow Master Thomas Kirke lacked the charm and good looks of Aeneas Sylvius and that his own legs were 'gey spindley'.

Sir Anthony Weldon was another seventeenth-century visitor ungallant enough to write: 'The beasts of Scotland are generally small – the women only excepted, of which there are none greater in the world.' His prejudice against Scotland and the Scots was wide and deep. 'They christen without the cross, marry without the ring, receive the sacrament without reverence, die without repentance, and bury without divine service.' The womenfolk he describes as being mere slaves, kept by jealous husbands in a state of subjection. But this opinion is contradicted by the fact that, during the insurrection of 1678, when Monmouth invited the Scots gentry to join the King's army, many of them who failed to respond gave as their excuse that their wives would not allow them to leave home and fight.

There were two English visitors, however, who did perceive admirable qualities in the ladies of North Britain.

In his *A Tour of Scotland* (1769) Thomas Pennant expresses some dismay at the servile condition of 'the female peasantry', but he further says that the townswomen 'fully emulate the character of the good wife so admirably described by Solomon'.

Another eighteenth-century tourist, Captain Burt, writing *Letters from a Gentleman in the North of Scotland*, declares that 'among the better sort there is a full proportion of pretty women', then adds a revealing postscript: 'Women, of course, grow handsomer and handsomer the longer one stays away from home.'

I have my own favourites among the ladies of Scotland.

Many a time, when sitting before a television camera, I have

wished Black Agnes of Dunbar could have been there beside
me, to add some zing to the programme. Her husband was the
tenth Earl of Dunbar and March. In 1334, while he was away
fighting for the Regent of Scotland, his countess was left in
charge of the castle. For five months she defended it against an
English force under the command of Montagu, Earl of Salisbury, during which time the castle was hemmed in by a cordon
of troops on land and two Genoese galleys out at sea.

With her dark complexion and long, flying hair, Agnes was a
born leader, brave and full of resource.

> She kept a stir in tower and trench,
> That brawling, boisterous Scottish wench.
> Came I early, came I late,
> I found Agnes at the gate.

When huge stones from the besiegers' catapults struck the
castle walls she would tell one of her women to go and wipe off
the dust with a white napkin. Then she would order arrows to
be sent sweeping down and the enemy would retreat, furious
and frustrated.

She was only twenty-five at the time. I can picture her in a
leather mini-skirt and swinging beads, striding the battlements,
brushing her hair out of her eyes and screaming defiance at the
English down below.

At one stage Salisbury tried to use a military engine called
'the sow'. This was a huge wooden shield, under cover of which
the English planned to advance and undermine the walls of the
castle. When Black Agnes saw it coming she laughed and
yelled:

> Beware, Montagow,
> For farrow shall thy sow!

And as she uttered this masterpiece of invective, if not of
poetry, her men dropped a boulder on top of the sow, and it
was smashed to pieces. The men underneath crawled out and

fled from the wreck. She shouted after them: 'I told you! A litter of squealing pigs, that's what you are!'

But in spite of her swash-buckling humour, she had a feminine sense of pity.

> Then to the Castle yard she sped,
> Where her worn troops in order stood.
> 'Spare all you can, my friends,' she said,
> 'Nor idly dip your dirks in blood.'

And at the end, when the castle was relieved by Sir Alexander Ramsay, her reaction was again feminine. She herself opened the gate to him. She rushed forward, flung her arms about his neck and began to cry.

Black Agnes was a real warrior. She lived to an old age, a strong supporter of the church. Her wild youth was no disadvantage.

In the seventeenth century, the ladies of the Scottish Covenant were remarkable characters. Their brave and unending faith was as inspiring as that of their menfolk: even as that of the Marquis of Argyll (a changed man after his villainous deeds at Dunaverty), who, on the night before he was executed for maintaining the Presbyterian faith, spoke quietly to a friend who had suggested suicide: 'I could die now like a Roman. But I choose rather to die tomorrow like a Christian.'

The sufferings inflicted on those women sound like African atrocities today.

Sir Robert Grierson, laird of Lagg, held burning matches between the fingers of young girls to make them betray their Covenanting fathers and brothers. General Dalziel threw women into pits containing frogs and snakes because they were loyal to their persecuted kinsmen or supplied hunted refugees with food.

The flag of Presbyterianism continued to fly, however, thanks in part to the courage and endurance of the ladies of the Covenant. A list of their names is like a roll of honour.

There was Jenny Geddes, who started the campaign against the English liturgy by hurling a stool at the Dean of Edinburgh's head. 'Wad ye say mass at my lug!' she shouted at him.

There was Lady Anne Cunningham, daughter of the seventh Earl of Glencairn and wife of the second Marquis of Hamilton, who, in 1639, personally opposed a fleet sent by King Charles I in an early effort to foist episcopacy on the Scots. She appeared on the seashore at Leith, mounted on a horse and carrying a pair of pistols loaded with bullets of gold, her idea being that leaden bullets were useless against the armour of the devil's agents.

There were Isabel Alison and Marion Harvey, who in 1681 were condemned to death in Edinburgh for attending 'field preachings' and commenting adversely on the cruelty of the soldiers. On the scaffold they joined in singing Psalm Thirteen, drowning the voice of the curate who had been ordered to preach to them. Marion Harvey was a domestic servant. She told the crowd that she was dying with a light heart. 'I am here today,' she said, 'for avowing Christ to be head of His Church. I sought Him and found Him. I found Him and will not let Him go!'

There were Margaret MacLachlan and Margaret Wilson, the Wigtown martyrs, who in 1685 were tied to stakes in the Solway and drowned as the water rose, stubbornly refusing to deny their religious beliefs. 'I am not afraid,' said Margaret Wilson. 'I am one of Christ's children.'

And there was Isobel Weir, the second wife of John Brown, a mild and harmless Ayrshireman who worked as a carter. One evening, on his way home, John was arrested by Claverhouse's dragoons. He was led into the house, where his wife and children were waiting. Claverhouse gave him a few minutes to prepare himself for death.

After saying his prayers, John turned to his wife and asked her if she were willing to part with him. 'I am willing,' she whispered.

'That is all I could wish,' he said. He gave her and the

children his blessing and told Claverhouse he was ready.

The dragoons held their fire. Perhaps John Brown's simple sincerity made them unwilling to murder him in cold blood. But Claverhouse – in the interests of military discipline, as he later explained – drew his own pistol and shot John Brown through the head.

'What do you think of your husband now?' he asked Isobel.

'I aye thocht muckle o' him,' she said. 'But never sae muckle as I do this day.'

The newspapers talk about violence – in this country and elsewhere – as if it were a modern phenomenon. In its name they create arguments which divide the people and divide the churches. But I reckon steadfast men, and perhaps more importantly, steadfast women will always have the last word.

To me, one of the most endearing of all the ladies of the Covenant was Lady Grizel Baillie, the story of whose life unfolds like a film script.

Grizel Hume was born on Christmas Day, 1665, eldest of the eighteen children of Sir Patrick and Lady Hume of Polwarth. As a girl of twelve she acted as juvenile undercover-agent, conveying secret messages between her father and Robert Baillie of Jerviswood, who, at the time, was in prison in Edinburgh. While carrying out this dangerous assignment she met George Baillie, Robert's son, and a love story began which out-Cartlands Barbara Cartland.

When Robert Baillie was executed for being implicated – allegedly – in the Rye House Plot, the Humes, as militant Covenanters, found themselves in trouble. Sir Patrick was denounced as a rebel. The Hume estates were forfeited and he went into hiding, his refuge being a vault in the parish kirk of Polwarth, a mile or so away from Redbraes Castle where the family lived. Every night Grizel faced the dark terrors of the churchyard to bring her father food, encouragement and gossip concerning happenings at home.

I can imagine some of the gossip dealt with her own difficulties in smuggling out his meals. For example, there was the time when troopers were in the castle, searching for Sir Patrick. With a view to taking it out later to give to her father, she had managed to hide the greater part of her dinner in her lap when suddenly one of her younger brothers began to draw the troopers' attention to what he imagined was his big sister's greed.

'Will you look at Grizel? While we've been supping our broth, she's eaten up a whole sheep's head!'

Fortunately the troopers were too busy to pay much attention to a small boy.

In the end, Sir Patrick and his family were forced to flee to Holland. Lady Hume was an invalid (no wonder, after having given birth to eighteen children), so Grizel made all the arrangements for the journey.

But this was not all. A week or so later she returned to Scotland to collect her little sister Gillian, who was ill and had been left behind. When the two girls landed at Brielle on the Dutch coast nobody was there to meet them. They had to walk to Rotterdam, and for most of the way Grizel carried her small sister on her back.

In Utrecht, where they finally settled, Grizel looked after the household, while her father earned a small income by practising as a doctor.

One day another Covenanting fugitive from Scotland arrived on their doorstep. He was George Baillie, who had never forgotten the 'wee Hume lassie' he'd met in Edinburgh. He stayed with the family for three and a half years, boisterous, gallant, head over heels in love with Grizel. He and Patrick, the young son of the house, enlisted together as guardsmen under the Prince of Orange.

Those years, according to Grizel, were the happiest of her life. Though the household was in poverty she sang at her work and even found time to write her own songs. Perhaps because her own love affair was happy and uncomplicated, these were often about tragic lovers:

When bonny young Johnny cam' ower the sea
He vowed he saw naething sae lovely as me.
He gi'ed me gowd rings and mony braw things –
An' werena my he'rt licht I wad dee.

But in this sad song the recurring last line does suggest something of Grizel's own patience, courage and good humour in face of all the 'slings and arrows of misfortune'.

Her story had a happy ending, which may be why it has never been made into a play for television. On the accession of William of Orange to the throne of Britain, her father's estates were returned to him. So were those of George Baillie, and in 1692 he and Grizel were married.

They had three children and lived in solid style, pillars of Kirk and State. But long afterwards, when she was a widow, still helping and looking after her numerous relatives, Lady Grizel told her daughter that she would have been quite content to live with her husband 'on bread and water on the top of a mountain'.

She was buried beside him on Christmas Day 1746.

Lady Grizel Baillie and Isobel Pagan had only one thing in common: they were both Scottish ladies.

Isobel was born in New Cumnock, Ayrshire, about 1741, and spent most of her life near Muirkirk. As a child she was deserted by her parents and brought up by 'a good religious old woman who lived a quiet, sober life'. Unfortunately, Isobel didn't follow her example.

She had a squint, went about on a crutch because of a lame leg, had several illegitimate children and drank so much that she was the envy of topers for miles around.

She lived in a kind of shelter beneath a stone archway, which had originally been a brick-store. To this 'howff' there came people from 'a' the airts' to drink illicit whisky and to hear her singing songs of her own composition. Her visitors included not only local miners and farm-workers but also many of the 'gentry' attracted by her wit – and potent liquor. In the month of August, when the grouse season began, shooting-tenants from England flocked to join the bacchanalian revels.

One sporting gentleman from across the Border persuaded her to enter a singing competition in an Ayr theatre. There, to the annoyance of the manager and the delight of her backer, she defeated the leading vocalist of a touring company which was performing in the theatre at the time. She had a lovely voice, and I have no doubt that today Hughie Green would have made her a shooting star in *Opportunity Knocks*.

She often attacked, verbally, the Church and its ministers. One day, passing the door of a tent in which an itinerant divine was preaching at length on some obscure question of theological doctrine, Isobel stopped to listen. After a while she stepped inside, nodded genially to the minister and said: 'Weel, still borin' awa', I see!' Then she departed, leaving both clergyman and congregation to regain breath.

Sometimes her attacks on people were physical. An Ayrshire laird who laughed at her squint was summarily felled by a blow from her crutch. If 'guests' appeared not to appreciate her 'hospitality' she would lay about her with the same weapon until they came to heel with apologies and gifts of money.

And yet, in spite of it all, Isobel Pagan had a genuine feeling for beauty and goodness. She knew her Bible from end to end and often quoted it to help her friends. The songs she composed and sang betray a wistful longing for what might have been, in other times and other circumstances.

Probably the best known of all her poems is 'Ca' the Yowes tae the Knowes'. Robert Burns admired it greatly and used it as the basis of a song of his own which begins, 'Hark the mavis' evening sang'. But the Pagan composition I like best is 'The Crook and Plaid', written in praise of a Lowland shepherd. Here is one of several verses:

> What though in storms o' winter part o' his flock should die,
> My laddie is aye cheerie and why should not I?
> The prospect o' the summer can weel mak' us gled,
> Contented is the laddie that wears the crook an' plaid.

Isobel Pagan died in 1821, and her funeral was attended by crowds from all over the country. When I think of her the words of a hymn come into my head: 'Say, poor sinner, lov'st thou me?'

There is one other Scottish lady for whom I have always had a great deal of sympathy and affection. For one thing, her maiden name was MacVicar, though her family and mine – as far as I know – were not connected. For another, she was a writer and published books, not because she felt inspired, with a message for the world, but because, like me, she was poor and badly needed the money. She was Mrs Grant of Laggan, whose *Letters from the Mountains* became famous in her own day.

Anne MacVicar was a soldier's daughter and spent most of her childhood in New York, where her father's regiment was stationed. As a girl her taste in reading was catholic: the Old Testament, which she read from end to end at the age of six; the rough and ready poems of Blind Harry and other bawdy Scottish minstrels; Milton's *Paradise Lost*, which she knew by heart before she was eight. I wonder what modern educationists would think of that lot.

In 1768 her father's health forced him back to Scotland, where he was appointed barrack-master at Fort Augustus. It was here that Anne met the Rev. James Grant when he became chaplain to the garrison. They fell in love at first sight. In 1779, soon after the Rev. James was inducted to the parish of Laggan, they were married.

Mrs Grant had learnt to speak Dutch in New York. Now she set about learning Gaelic, in order to help her husband in the parish. She also kept up a regular correspondence with friends across the world and wrote numerous poems and songs, perhaps the most famous of which is 'Oh where, tell me where is my Highland laddie gone?'. How she found time to do all this balks my imagination, because in the meantime she was presenting her husband with twelve children.

Then the scourge of those unhealthy days struck the family. Four of her children died of consumption; and finally her

husband died, too, of the same disease. She was left a homeless
and penniless widow with eight children to keep.

For a while she tried farming, living in a cottage lent to her
by the Duke of Gordon. But this was a failure, and once more
freezing poverty came limping round the corner.

As a last resort somebody suggested that she should publish
her poems, and friends gathered round to finance the project.
When the book came out the *Edinburgh Review*, seldom flatter-
ing, described her verses as having 'beauty, tenderness and
delicacy', and a first edition of 3000 copies quickly sold out.
Mrs Grant was back in business.

She went to live in Stirling, but her family troubles were
still pressing. And tragic. One by one her children died, with the
exception of her youngest son; and it was to pay doctors' bills
that she collected some of her letters to her friends and made a
book of them. In this she was encouraged by Wordsworth and
Mrs Hemans, amongst others, and in 1806 *Letters from the
Mountains* was published. It was an immediate success, in this
country and in America, and other books followed.

Eventually Mrs Grant went to live in Edinburgh. As a young
woman she had been tall, slender and good-looking. Now she
fell downstairs and broke her leg, and as she grew older, without
much exercise, she became heavy and stiff. But she made a joke
of her stoutness and played hostess to many literary lions,
among them Sir Walter Scott.

'I think Mr Scott's appearance very unpromising and com-
monplace,' she wrote, demonstrating feminine honesty of a
high order. 'Yet though no gleam of genius animates his
countenance, much of it appears in his conversation, which is
rich, easy, various and animated.'

And what did Sir Walter think of Mrs Grant? 'She is proud
as a Highlandwoman, vain as a poetess, but she merits regard
by her firmness and elasticity of mind with which she has borne
a succession of great domestic calamities.'

I don't suppose many people today have read *Letters from
the Mountains*. I think it is a book of great charm, written by

one who not only loved nature and humanity but also possessed a rare gift for portraying Scottish life and character. When its author, in her old age, applied for a pension, her friends organized a supporting petition. In this they described her writings as 'addressing themselves to the national pride of the Scottish people and breathing at once a spirit of patriotism and of that candour which renders patriotism unselfish and liberal'.

Mrs Grant lived to the age of eighty-four. She died on 7 November 1838 and was buried in St Cuthbert's churchyard in Edinburgh.

Where did she find the courage to challenge the stormy world and sail determinedly through it? 'I read a chapter of the Bible every day,' she said. 'It helps me to face sorrow and triumph with equal fortitude.'

Anne Grant, as one MacVicar to another, as one writer to another, I salute you.

St Columba preached that women should be raised high on a pedestal of reverence, reminding men of the dignity of motherhood exemplified by Mary. Today the Church of Scotland remembers his words. Prejudice against woman ministers and elders is fading. The influence of women in the church is growing stronger. This, to me, is encouraging.

In the human situation it is wives and mothers, not officials of the state, who are in a key position to influence the moral and physical health of the coming generations. I believe that the tensions and strains of modern living, including the 'frustrations' of young people reared on a glib philosophy of 'take' rather than of 'give', all stem from a lack of faith in the family unit, which, in turn, leads to a lack of faith in the community as a whole. Women, by their example, have the best opportunity to bring about a resurgence of this faith. Through discipline and love they can demonstrate – like Black Agnes of Dunbar, like Lady Grizel Baillie, like Mrs Grant of Laggan and all the rest – that the family unit is the principal source of strength and happiness in any community.

They are the dreamers of happy dreams for their children and, by the same token, better placed than anyone else to give practical expression to those dreams.

St Columba's mother was Eithne, of the ruling house of Leinster. While she was awaiting the birth of her son she dreamt that an angel came to her, bringing a filmy garment, 'in which the most beautiful colours of all the flowers seemed to be portrayed'. She held it in her hands, amazed by its beauty; but almost at once the angel took it from her and allowed the soft breeze to fill it out and carry it away. Eithne saw it expanding until 'its measurement was larger than the mountains and the forests'. She was sad at losing it, but the angel comforted her. 'You are about to become the mother of a son who shall blossom for heaven and be of so beautiful a character that he shall be reckoned among his own people as one of the prophets.'

At this point I remember something my mother used to say: 'Why emphasize the differing roles of men and women? Surely we're all simply human beings, with equal rights and privileges?'

The Padre had no ready answer. Neither have I. So, in male humility, I will abandon the subject and, as they say, 'let that flee stick tae the wa' '.

10

The Ringing Grooves of Change

The stubby mountain crests on either side are less than half a mile apart. In Southend we call it the Gap. As a stranger approaches the place, on foot or in a car, he may imagine it to be a gateway at the end of the world, with nothing beyond it but the shimmer of *Tir nan Og*, the Hebridean land of the ever young. Here the narrow road leaps out over a crag and ricochets down for a dizzy 1500 feet to the Mull of Kintyre Lighthouse and the sea.

Here also John Leitch, coastguard turned shepherd, once saw an object, glowing and hovering between the crests, which he believed to be a flying saucer.

'It was in the twilight of an autumn evening,' John told a local reporter, brought by me to meet him in the Keil Hotel bar. 'There was no wind, and as I walked along the road towards the Gap I could see the sky between the mountain crests like a greyish-blue stage backdrop. The first thing I noticed was a sound – a kind of thin, rushing sound, as if a small wind had sprung up beyond the Mull. But there was no wind, and I got a strange feeling: like being surrounded by strangers. Then I saw it, hovering about fifty feet above the road-sign in the Gap. An elliptical object, dark against the sky, but with light pouring from what seemed to me like portholes. Somehow I wasn't afraid, but there was a prickling in my body, as if the air was full of electricity. I looked round behind me to see if there was anything else in the sky. There wasn't. When I faced the Gap again the object had disappeared. The only feeling I had then was one of loneliness.'

He was a good journalist, that local reporter. His rendering in print of John's occasionally blasphemous words is almost poetic and does full justice to Southend's only story about an Unidentified Flying Object. It happened nearly twenty years ago, and today only a few of us remember. We have more practical things to worry about.

On a day in 1975 Jean and I stood in the Gap, there at the Mull. Behind us the purple heather and the dry peat hags, a protest of grouse calls and an acrid scent of autumn in the air. Before us, distantly down and making our heads swim like the heads of hovering astronauts, a crawling plain of sea, pale blue like the sky and decorated with patterns composed of tides and currents. Eleven miles away, across the Channel, a basking sea monster called Rathlin, and beyond Rathlin the cliffs of Torr Head on the coast of Antrim.

In the space above it all a golden eagle soared, attended on each majestic glide and turn by a little bird flying beneath him.

Jean handed me the binoculars. '*Could* be a wren, I suppose, as in some of the stories.'

A legend that the king of birds has a valet which accompanies him even into the eye of the sun is found in many cultures, including the Gaelic, the German and the Greek. But since that day Jean and I have never found an expert 'bird man' who can identify its species. When we describe what we saw the experts look at us in much the same way, I suppose, as we looked at John Leitch when he told his tale of the flying saucer. They shake their heads, as statesmen do at poets.

The great bird and his friend disappeared beyond the mountain crest on our left. I turned the binoculars on to the sea and saw something else to cause questions and excitement. A small grey ship, miles away under the Irish coast, stationary and sinister.

'Another one,' I said.

For the past few years we have seen them: the little survey ships, prospecting for oil. Sometimes they are visible from our dining-room window, moving slowly up and down the North Channel, which, in Gaelic is called *Struth-na-Maoile*.

According to the geologists, coal exists beneath the North Channel. A seam snakes out from Machrihanish, where there used to be a pit, across to the open-cast workings around Ballycastle. And – so runs the greedy word – where there is coal there may be oil.

Another legend relates that seven tides meet at the Mull of Kintyre. They spill east from the Atlantic, south from the Minches and north from the Irish Sea and the Firth of Clyde. From the Gap they are plainly to be seen, smooth patches of azure water fringed with ragged white lace. A dangerous place for small boats – though in kindly weather Archie Cameron lays and lifts lobster creels close in along the rock-piled shore. But to men who can establish oil-rigs in the turbulent North Sea, seven fast tides present no problem.

Jean and I stood beside the painted sign:

DANGER
This hill is dangerous
Vehicular traffic
prohibited, except on lighthouse business

But the danger of the vertiginous road was not the danger we had in mind.

We saw, in imagination, a small forest of oil-rigs sprouting around the Mull, turning *Tir nan Og* into a paradise lost. We heard a cacophony of hammers at an oil platform construction yard on the Kintyre coast, harsh sounds to frighten away for ever the eagles and the flying saucers. We smelt the stink of oil from a refinery. It irritated the lungs and overwhelmed the scents of the heather and the wild thyme.

That day, as Jean and I contemplated 'progress', our mood became sour. Was this an instinctive reaction of old squares to the intrusion of new values? Or was it the result of fear that our country way of life was coming near an end and that we might find it difficult to adjust to an urban ethos?

As we left the Gap and drove away along the mountain road, back to Achnamara, we decided that our sense of proportion might be awry. To visiting friends – and to ourselves – life at the Mull of Kintyre appears attractively quiet and uneventful; but throughout the centuries hasn't it always been disturbed by excitement and change?

In the evening, after a supper of flounders – speared that afternoon by a friendly young visitor from the caravan park and left on our doorstep – I went outside, stood in the garden and tried to think.

Thinking, for me, is not an easy process. All my life, as the creator of books, plays, films and even strip cartoons, I have had to keep flogging a lazy mind into action. When the mood takes me I would much rather climb to the Gap and watch the eagles, dig in my garden and see the turnips grow, play golf and shoot a scratch 66, make tender love and forget the place and the time – I would much rather *do* all these things than write about them. But the time comes when 'a man's gotta do what a man's gotta do'.

First, I asked myself a question. Are you and Jean afraid of change? The answer came clear enough. We are afraid of change, not so much in the environment as in the Scots people and in ourselves.

When ambition ran strong, I used to visit London twice a year, flying first over the Firth of Clyde, then down and away across the 'coloured counties' into the confusion of Heathrow. Nowadays, taking account of air fares, hotel bills and a minimum of 'extras', a trip to London lasting forty-eight hours would cost me more than £100. In the jargon of the accountants, this, for a writer, is no longer 'economically viable'.

In London I talked with editors and publishers, sometimes alone, sometimes shepherded by an axious agent. If book sales were satisfactory I was entertained in a style far above my domestic station, in expensive restaurants near Piccadilly and in temporarily fashionable ones around Soho. If business languished, and my mission was the peddling of new ideas, I did the entertaining, advised and instructed by my agent. This always caused a long-suffering banker in Campbeltown to make threatening noises on my return. But I enjoyed those visits. They were exciting therapy for a lone author with heather in his ears.

I love the people of London. Professionally and socially they have always been kind to me. I know, of course, that in the Scots idiom they can 'see me coming': in appearance, manner and dress an unsophisticated Hebridean from Kintyre is naturally different from bred-in-the-bone Londoners, and the difference becomes even more obvious when I talk.

I am sure that most of the people I used to meet were inspired by a feeling of warm protectiveness, no doubt similar to that which they might experience on encountering a lost and inarticulate native of Basutoland. Shop assistants and waitresses listened earnestly to my requests. They smiled and called me 'love', speaking slowly as if to a child; and once, when I tried to walk through a confectioner's glass door, they rushed anxiously to help, soothing my hurt in clucking Cockney. Editors and publishers called for their assistants to come and inspect me, while my agent – who, for children's books, happens to be a lady – did her best to make capital out of curiosity. But I never felt uneasy or shy. The natives were friendly and did their best to make me feel at home. I hoped that if ever I met a Londoner benumbed by bagpipes, whisky and the Gaelic at a midnight ceilidh in Argyll I would offer him the same compassionate regard.

On a human level my friends and acquaintances in London were – and still are – lovely people. Sometimes, however, I felt that they were puzzled by certain aspects of my 'Scottishness'.

One day I sat in a publisher's office in Bloomsbury. My agent was telling a tale, substantially true, concerning the success of my stories in Scotland.

Harold, the publisher, said: 'Success in Scotland means nothing here. This is where the action is. This is where you learn to command big sales. Why on earth don't you live in London?'

In Madagascar, during the Second World War, I had a friend, the chief of Ivovona village. If I asked him an embarrassing question – or one he found difficult to answer – he would spit out some ochre-tinted leaf juice, raise his eyes and murmur: 'The truth is with Zanahary!' (Which, being translated into Scots, means 'God kens!') Not being a chewer of exotic leaves, nor pious like my Malagasy friend, I merely raised my eyes and, in answer to Harold's question, gave a Heath heave of the shoulders.

'Let's face it,' he went on, 'you're out of touch up there among the seals and the seagulls. You haven't a hope of capturing the market if you don't mix with people – all kinds of people, good, bad and indifferent. Here in London you'd come alive. You'd learn what living really means.'

I am not good at providing *extempore* answers to an argument. Ideas careened about in my head like bingo numbers. I wanted to tell Harold that I did mix with people, good, bad and indifferent: perhaps not so much with sophisticated townsfolk but with people all the same. I wanted to tell him that in Scotland I felt intensely alive, with the wind and the rain and sunlit golf courses as tonic nerve restorers, while in London a certain numbness came over my spirit and it was difficult for me to distinguish the wood among so many trees. I wanted to make a humorous remark accusing Harold of being only half-alive because he was out of touch with seals and seagulls. But the ideas failed to become words and all I said was: 'I don't think I could write in London. I couldn't be myself.'

The truth is, I was afraid of change, as I knew Jean would be if a move to London were contemplated. This is why Achnamara has remained our home base since we married in 1936.

I am glad to notice that our son Jock has the same instinct. Though for the past eighteen years he has worked as a sports writer with the *Scottish Daily Express* and owns a bachelor 'pad' in Glasgow, he comes home whenever an opportunity presents itself. We will keep Achnamara warm for him. Some day, in the future, he may retire to it.

That evening, in Achnamara garden, I asked myself a second question. *Why* are we afraid of change? In a lucid moment the answer became clear. We are afraid of change because, like the crofters of Sollas, we equate it with being uprooted from the people and the physical environment we know and understand. Uprooted and replanted in a more luxurious London – or elsewhere furth of Scotland – we could never tell when our spirit might wither and finally die.

For Londoners and other urban people, dreaming of a life in the country 'away from it all', the same answer may apply in reverse.

So my thinking had led me to a fairly obvious conclusion. Jean and I were Scots of the Scots. Like most of our neighbours, we were heirs to an ancient heritage, and, without evidence of that heritage around us – the rocks in our Scotch – it was difficult to imagine us existing at all. But I saw plainly enough that, in a manner of speaking, there was no future in clinging too stubbornly to the past. Jean and I should have to face up to and, in our own way, come to terms with progress.

But as George Hutcheon used to say – he was our head teacher of mathematics at Campbeltown Grammar School – a conclusion always requires a definition. In this case my problem was the definition of 'progress'.

I believe good progress has been made in providing better food for more people, better housing for the less affluent, broader bands of education for adolescents and adults, more sophisticated medicine for the sick, more efficient safeguards against crime and corruption. Today, especially for young people and old people, life is much happier than it was, say, a hundred years ago.

But is it progress, in the sense of going forward, when crofters and farmers leave their ploughs and fishermen their nets to work instead at an assembly line? Is it progress when half a dozen employees of a car firm, in the name of egalitarianism, can go on strike and so render 100000 of their 'brothers' unemployed? Is it progress when cities are built larger and larger (and fields and forests, in consequence, become smaller and smaller) and we drive in our cars through artificial canyons, bumper to bumper, inhaling exhaust fumes which are far more dangerous to health than those of tobacco? Is it progress when new weapons are invented to kill more people at longer range, when a little man – in every sense of the word – is given the opportunity to depress a nuclear switch in America or Russia or China and bring the world to an abrupt end?

For many of us, life seems to have become so drearily complicated that it can be made bearable only by using a television set to avoid reality. Are we all so mentally tired that we must allow 'the box' to do most of our thinking for us? More and better television is equated with progress. Surely, however, the quality of man's mental processes is infinitely more important than advances in methods of communication.

And what about man's physical processes? Gaping at all the advertisements which accompany 'entertainment' on the goggle box, are we not in danger of being brain-washed into eating and drinking and smoking a lot of dangerous rubbish?

Good progress has been made in education.

Until comparatively recent times the chief source of education in Scotland was the Church, before and after the Reformation. John Knox was more than a churchman: he was also a schoolmaster, whose stated purpose was to establish 'a school in every town and a school-master in every parish', so that all children, rich or poor, might have an education 'according to their capacity'. Like many other country places, Southend benefited from an application of this philosophy. At one time – less than a hundred years ago – it had three schools. Now it has only one.

But progress in education has always been hampered by politics.

In John Knox's day the men of power were the nobility and the big landowners, who were afraid that servants and labourers might be hard to find if too many people were educated, afraid that an advance in education might bring about an erosion of their own privilege. Consequently they did their utmost to delay the full flowering of Knox's ideal.

In 1872 education became the responsibility of the State rather than of the Church, and the men of power became the politicians and the bureaucrats. At the present time the stultifying arguments concern state versus private, comprehensive versus grammar, the status and payment of teachers, the perennial challenge of youth to age and experience. And once again, it seems to me, the essence of education – the intimate dialogue between teachers and the taught, the care and nurture of young minds – is liable to be overlooked.

Enormous sums are being spent on fancy subjects – on batteries of gas and electric cookers, on tools and materials which would do credit to a shipyard, on bigger and better television sets, on special buses for pupils who must learn to swim but who have forgotten how to walk. Enormous sums are being spent on sociological investigations, the results of which could be forecast free of charge by any sensible teacher or parent.

The whole situation reminds me of the country minister who one Sunday, during a spell of dry weather, prayed for rain for the farmers. Sure enough, during the week it rained incessantly, from morning to night. The following Sunday he got up in the pulpit, and, in reproving tones, prayed again: 'O Lord, I know that last Sunday we prayed for rain, but this is ridiculous!'

In all the turmoil of innovation I think young minds are still in danger of being neglected. Subjects included in the fancy side of education are all splendid in their own way, but are they educative in the true sense? Is it progress that they should be crowded into a school curriculum at the expense of the Three Rs, of the humanities, of modern languages (including the Gaelic), of the sciences, of modern studies and, above all, of history and English (and Scottish) language and literature?

Certainly all these ancillary subjects should be dealt with in good schools, but, it seems to me, only in a minor way, to reinforce basic training in the home, by parents. Then more attention could be given to the real work of educating young minds and money saved with which to improve teachers' salaries.

Instead of our 'welfare' society being kind to its young – which in all charity, I am sure is its intention – has it not become as cruel as the noblemen and landowners of John Knox's day? Are some short-sighted parents and teachers not aiding and abetting in this cruelty, encouraging take instead of give, encouraging this disastrous, anti-social modern concept that each child should be allowed to 'do his own thing'?

Teachers who really have a care for children – they are still in the majority, though perhaps an increasingly silent majority – are those who insist on discipline and the values of authority.

'But what,' it may be said, 'can you do with the kind of children we have today?' This is a valid point, though when I hear parents griping about the lack of discipline in schools I always want to ask what they themselves are doing about it at home, where discipline should begin. But I don't think that either parents or teachers should blame the children.

'The young people of today love luxury. They have bad manners, contempt for authority and disrespect for their elders. They no longer get up when old people enter the room. They contradict their parents, wolf their food and tyrannize their teachers.'

Who said this? Malcolm Muggeridge? Robin Day? The Rector of Glasgow High School? Not so. It was Socrates, another well-known headmaster, who, incidentally, got so steamed up about his apparent lack of success with children that he took an overdose and died in 399 BC.

The nature of children doesn't change, only the philosophical and political climates in which they live. At the moment, it seems to me, we are threatened by an ice age.

A teacher's sacred duty, according to one school of sociology, is to restore youth's faith in the older generation. To this end he must be unfailingly reasonable, totally unbiased, open to cultural innovation and undismayed by personal hostility. Thesociologists don't explain how this is supposed to prepare the young for a world that can be relied upon to display none of these characteristics. Nor do they explain why such a burden should be put upon teachers alone, with no mention of parents, who surely have the prime responsibility.

My own idea of a teacher's sacred duty is that he should endeavour to establish in young minds not only knowledge and how to use it but also a higher concept of living, an ideal of discipline, with love and full consideration for other human beings. And surely the best way he can do this is by personal example.

In the church today there are clergymen who go to great lengths trying to be with it, pandering to what they imagine is a modern youthful taste in music, clothes, permissiveness. The Padre had a name for them: 'blasted mountebanks'. I think there are some trendy teachers who try to do the same, who try to become popular by glorifying the idea that youth must always be allowed to do its own thing. The tragedy is that such clergymen and teachers nearly always fail, discovering, often too late, that popularity and respect can be acquired only in the long term, when their congregations and their pupils have learned to appreciate that ethics and education have unchanging standards: standards laid down long ago for the benefit of society as a whole.

I remember my sister Rona telling me how one day she met another lady teacher coming along a corridor in Campbeltown Grammar School. In one hand she carried a Bible, in the other a strap. 'There you are, Rona,' she said: 'the foundations of Scottish education!' It could be argued that the Bible and the strap are twin symbols of discipline, spiritual and physical. Has Scottish education improved so much since they went out of fashion?

Robert Louis Stevenson summed up teaching in two lines:

> Lord, thy most pointed pleasure take
> And stab my spirit broad awake.

The word 'stab' infers a measure of pain, in the sense of hard discipline, and I reckon modern society is inclined to shy away from pain as a therapeutic agent. There is pain in real education. Is it progress to shy away from that, too?

Good progress has also been made in medicine. But again, is it not progress almost entirely in a material sense?

It has been pointed out to me that the boundaries of medicine are precise, that the art of medicine is the diagnosis and treatment of diseases of the body due to physical causes. But is this not as narrow a vision of medicine as Calvinism is of Christianity, as the science of statistics is of modern philosophy? I believe that real progress in medicine must encompass not only a developing knowledge of science but also a developing knowledge of integrated humanity – of what Neil Munro used to call 'the strange cantrips of the human heart'.

When he retired during the Second World War, Dr James Niven had been practising in Southend for more than fifty years. He brought Jock into the world, charging me three guineas for a long night's work, and his proud boast was that in all his professional career he never lost a baby. Dr Jim, as we called him, was typical of the old-fashioned country doctor. 'Keep warm and take an aspirin' was his panacea for many ills.

He was frank and friendly. If Old Roderick had an ingrowing toe-nail Dr Jim cut it out, either in Old Roderick's bedroom or in his own firelit surgery. Then he advised his patient not to be a vain old so-and-so but to wear boots a size larger in future. As nature completed the cure Old Roderick had an enjoyable time informing his long-suffering family and village-corner cronies about his 'operation'.

Modern medicine tends to treat Old Roderick in an entirely different way. Every resource of science is deployed for his physical benefit, but his need for spiritual solace is apt to be ignored.

In many areas of Scotland – though not, I am thankful to say, in Southend – Dr Jim has become Dr Who, a faceless member of a group practice and a comparative stranger to Old

Roderick. He examines the suppurating toe in silence and with apparent indifference. He fills in a number of suspicious-looking forms, then summons an ambulance – in certain circumstances even an air-ambulance – and Old Roderick is lugged away from his family and cronies into a distant hospital, to him a cathedral of dreadful mysteries. Nobody tells him what's going on or even what's wrong with him. Great machines are wheeled in to probe and X-ray the offending toe, and poor Old Roderick – to the scientists a mere number on a card – spends hours of anxiety, homesick and lonely, imagining that he has gangrene or foot and mouth disease – and that in any case his leg is going to be amputated.

Eventually his toe is cured – of course it is: after all, we're in the last quarter of the twentieth century – but his nerves are shattered. He is lucky if he escapes at last without being taken into care by lurking psychiatrists.

Could all this commotion and worry for a patient not be avoided if GPs in general and hospital doctors in particular were encouraged to act like human beings, not as diagnostic rubber stamps subservient to the twin gods of group practice and specialist science?

I have a vision of what may happen in the near future, if medicine continues to progress only in scientific terms. I see a Prime Minister with Margaret Thatcher's brain, Jim Callaghan's heart, Enoch Powell's lungs and Michael Foot's liver, with rib-cage by Universal Skeletons Limited and legs and arms by Road Crashes Unlimited. In the heat of parliamentary debate this monster seethes and bubbles and finally blows up in our faces. And why? Because as yet no doctor has enough skill and understanding to help it acquire a coherent personality. Because, instead of 'Onward, Christian soldiers', the slogan now seems to be 'Onward, Christian Barnard'.

Of course, all this is exaggerated – I am not a practising journalist for nothing – and entirely unfair to the good and dedicated doctors who make up the great majority of the medical profession. But it is on the good and dedicated doctors that we must rely to guide progress in medicine along human as well as scientific channels. I am convinced that doctors should never detach themselves from humanity any more than ministers of religion should detach themselves from politics, any more than politicians should detach themselves from the spiritual as opposed to the economic needs of their constituents.

So, out there in the garden, I came to an end of my think about progress. I had found a definition – a vague definition which I realized could be satisfactory only to myself (and perhaps to Jean) a definition which depended a good deal on my belief that progress should be built upon tried and tested spiritual values, such as those of Christianity.

It had, however, cleared my mind of sourness in regard to imaginary oil-rigs at the Mull of Kintyre. It showed me plainly that our parish of Southend, being a microcosm of Scotland, is constantly liable to upheavals in thought and action, for which even the coming of the black, black oil represents only a small tremor in the graph of time.

11

What about that Parish Pump?

The Padre believed that in spite of the many wrong turnings we take at times, the spiritual and physical condition of humanity is slowly improving. During quiet intervals I think so, too. Nuclear disaster may threaten. Some groups in society may lose discipline and become softly permissive. The oil industry may have an ugly side to it. Education and medicine may take curious twists. But all the time, as we continue to emerge from temporary clouds of fog, we are getting nearer the sunlight. I disagree with an erudite friend of mine at Edinburgh University who equates human progress with the labour of Sisyphus, the King of Corinth who, for his sins, was banished to Hades, condemned for ever to push a block of marble up a hill, only for it to roll back down again each time.

Sometimes, as I contemplate the hurly-burly of clashing desires and ideologies, the situation does appear Sisyphean to me. Not long ago I read about an area of green fused sand uncovered in the Arabian desert: green fused sand which, though hundreds of thousands of years old, was exactly similar to that found in New Mexico after the explosion of the first experimental A-bomb. My flesh did a cold creep. But then it occurred to me that even though my imaginings might have validity, my mind was much too finite to grasp the whole picture. Perhaps this was a sealed loft I wasn't supposed to try and open. Better to mind my own simple business and concentrate on lofts of lesser mystery.

My publisher, guide and good friend, Gerald Austin, once said to me: 'When you reach the age of about eighty and have become a doyen of Scottish letters' – 'That would be like Willie Hamilton becoming a member of the Privy Council!' I interjected – 'when you reach that stage, Angus, then you can write a book of mystic philosophy. At present you tell stories better than you philosophize. So keep on telling stories.' Then, pursuing English logic to a canny conclusion, he added: 'They pay better.'

It sounds like something my practical mother might have said, and I am grateful for the advice and for the discipline such advice imposes. But behind the gratitude, behind the image I endeavour to present of a hard-headed professional writer, there is a Hebridean mystic – perhaps a kind of latter-day Brahan Seer – struggling to get out. The Padre would have understood. I think Jean and Jock and my brothers understand, too. And suffer with patience the moody results.

In this book I have essayed a compromise, using stories to reveal some of the background details which have shaped my Scottish way of living and thinking: some of the rocks which are ingredients in my Scotch, important to me, if perhaps to nobody else. The result may be incoherent, but in its very incoherence I believe it presents a relevant picture.

I remember once being greeted at Achnamara front door by a stranger, who said he had been watching me on television. 'My goodness,' he went on, looking me up and down, 'you're a big man. Seeing you on the goggle box I thought you were a dwarf with ulcers!' It may be that the writing in *Rocks in My Scotch* creates the same effect as a television tube. If so, I have no gripe. Truth, like beauty, is in the eye of the beholder.

There are many other rocks which to me are of importance.

I remember St Andrew, who wasn't a Scot at all but, according to some scholars, a Russian.

The legend is that St Regulus, otherwise St Rule, landed in Fife from Europe with relics of St Andrew: 'an arm-bone, three fingers, a tooth and a knee-pan'. The date of this happening is uncertain, estimates ranging from the fourth century to the eighth. But it gave Scotland a patron saint and a beautiful town:

St Andrews, a miniature of cultural Scotland with its history, religion, education – and golf.

It also gave us St Andrew's Night, on 30 November, when we eat haggis, sing 'Scots Wha Hae' with suitable fervour and raise our glasses to 'auld lang syne'. On this night we are the great folk, proud, independent, free.

But on the following day we face not only a hang-over but also reality. We go back to 'auld claes an' parritch', to competing for a living as we try to sell oil and coal and steel, ships and cars and oil-rigs to the Americans, the Germans, the Russians, the Chinese – and, of course, the English. On 30 November we are 'Jock Tamson's bairns'. Next day we realize once more that Jock Tamson's bairns are international.

On St Andrew's Night we toast the thistle and the motto that goes with it: *'Nemo me impune lacessit'*, 'Nobody affronts me without getting hurt'. Perhaps this is one reason why the English call us, at times, intolerant and even arrogant. But the English – especially the southern English – should remember that our memory of oppression is much more recent than theirs.

There was Flodden, when the young Scots king and his still younger soldiers – 'the floo'ers o' the forest' – were 'a' wede awa' '. There was Glencoe, when innocent men were slain in the snow on orders from London. There were the redcoats after Culloden and the savage Clearances, when the people's homes and lives were sacrificed on the altar of higher profits for the landowners. There was the martyrdom of the unemployed on Clydeside and elsewhere between the wars, an echo of which seems to be occurring even now.

This is why some of us have a thistle complex. Flodden and Glencoe, the Clearances and the 'Hungry Twenties' are not such ancient history. They can still cause prickly reaction against any threat, real or imaginary, to our chosen way of life. The memories of injustices in the new countries of Africa will not easily be forgotten either.

We are, however, aware of our problem. If Scotland is to be worth living in and worth enjoying, like our coloured brothers we must forgive and remember only with objectivity. Instead of being inward-looking, jealously guarding our pride, we must try to give something, to share our ideals with the world.

We have plenty to give.

I remember Bannockburn.

There they stood on the morning of 24 June 1314, 7000 Scots inspired by the love of freedom against 25000 feudal mercenaries of the King of England. Behind them the dark mountains of their homeland. In front, along the banks of the burn, the glittering panoply of the English army, 'banners right fairly flaming, and pencels to the wind waving'.

Before the battle the Scots knelt on the ground while a passage from the Bible was read by the Abbot of Inchaffray. 'Comfort ye, comfort ye, my people.' Then they listened to his prayer: 'Deliver us, O Lord, from our enemies and from the hands of those that hate us.'

From the low ground Edward II saw them on their knees. He laughed. 'They are afraid! Will such men fight?' But his adherent, the Earl of Angus, who knew his countrymen, shook his head gravely and answered: 'Your Majesty, they will fight. Those men are not afraid.'

Suddenly the Scots attacked: the men of Strathclyde and the Borders under Sir James Douglas; the men of Ross and Inverness under Thomas Randolph, Earl of Moray; the men of Buchan and Mar and Lennox under the King's brother, Edward. Bruce himself commanded the reserve, his own tenantry from Carrick and the clansmen from Argyle and the Isles.

The English were trapped between the rising waters of the Forth and the Bannock burn, so that their superior strength could not be deployed; and the battle swung decisively when Bruce called upon Aonghas Og, MacDonald of the Isles, to rally his men and charge the English flank. 'My hope is constant in thee,' he said, words that can still be found on the Clanranald coat of arms. Finally the *coup de grâce* was delivered by the 'small folk', the farmers, the fishermen, the clerks and the weavers, the ordinary people for whose liberties Bruce was fighting.

I am proud not so much concerning the outcome of the battle but that before it the Scots were not ashamed to pray. (It is sad to record that like Cromwell's troops in England 300 years later, who were also not afraid to pray, they went on to fight and kill and maim with savage enthusiasm. Why? What lies behind this particular sealed door?)

I am proud to remember, too, that only seven years after Bannockburn, in 1320, the clergymen and people of Scotland sent a remarkable letter to the Pope. It is now called the Arbroath Declaration.

For centuries any reference to this document was suppressed. Some years ago, in London, I spoke about it to a gathering of English writers. Few of them had ever heard of it. The passage from it most often quoted runs as follows: 'While there exist a hundred of us we will never submit to England. We fight not for glory, wealth or honour but for that liberty without which no virtuous man shall survive.'

But there is another passage which for me is equally magnificent: 'Should he [Bruce] abandon our cause or aim at reducing us or our kingdom, we will instantly expel him as a common enemy, and, under God, choose another King.'

It is hard to believe that such words were written while Robert the Bruce was at the height of his power and popularity. I look upon them as a trumpet call by Christians, echoing down the years: a trumpet call for democracy.

Frequently I have been told by my English friends that I am a typical Scot. I try to explain that there is no such animal.

To begin with, a typical Scottish accent doesn't exist. Some Highlanders have a musical lilt. Some Lowlanders are broad and deliberate. Glasgow has an accent which is often as difficult to understand as London's Cockney. My own is unique, a weird mixture of Highland, Lowland and Irish.

And what about the Scottish character? Highlanders are supposed to be either carefree and energetic or sad and lazy, according to their mood. Lowlanders and East Coasters are supposed to be dour and hard-working, tight-fisted and lacking in humour. Like all generalizations this is entirely misleading. Highlanders can be dour and Lowlanders carefree, and East Coasters can be full of fun. (In the Hebrides, where there are no trains to catch, I must admit that nobody pays much attention to the clock.)

The legend of Scottish meanness, including corny jokes about the streets of Aberdeen being deserted on a flag-day, is also misleading. In general we are a thrifty race, the result of nagging poverty in the past. But I think we can claim to be reasonably hospitable, to our neighbours and to strangers. We give foreigners a genuine if sometimes cautious welcome, and I have never encountered in Scotland anything like a colour bar.

Kushi Mohammed, born in Pakistan, comes into our homes to sell his drapery and have a cup of tea, and we return the visit to sample his curry and chapattis. There is not the slightest embarrassment on either side. Kushi is a Scot now, like the rest of us.

It may be said, however, that our hospitality is not always purely altruistic. Some of us make a handsome living looking after strangers, encouraged by the Tourist Board.

There was an old lady in Kintyre who gave board and lodging to a famous artist. Before he left he showed her a painting he had made of her cottage and the glen behind it. 'This will be hung in a London gallery,' he said. 'Thousands of people will see it. You've been so good to me that now I'd like to return the compliment. Is there anything special you'd like me to add to the picture – a tree or a bush, your favourite flowers, for example?' 'Oh, *chiall*,' she said, 'I'm not sure if there's anything really. But since you're kind enough to ask – and since it will be seen by so many people – maybe you could be putting a wee notice in the window of the cottage there: "To let for August"?'

I don't believe that as Scots we are particularly mean, though, of course, we have no monopoly of hospitality. London has the reputation of being cold and aloof, but my personal experience is that Londoners are as kind and generous to a stranger as any people in the world.

In Scotland, however, we have an advantage. We have a heritage from St Columba, who, while in Iona, wrote this poem:

> I saw a stranger yestreen:
> I put food in the eating-place,
> Music in the listening-place;
> And in the sacred name of the Trinity,
> He blessed myself and my house,
> My cattle and my dear ones,
> And the lark said in her song,
> Often, often, often goes the Christ
> In the stranger's guise.

Another legend is that we are a parochial lot in Scotland, thirled to the parish pump, for ever bolstering up our ego with songs like 'Hail, Caledonia!' and 'Scotland the Brave'. There may be some truth in it, but I believe that everybody is touched with tar from the same brush. What could be more parochial than 'Maybe it's because I'm a Londoner?' What more perfervidly nationalistic than 'Land of Hope and Glory'?

I think there is a question here as to whether pride in one's own parish is such a bad thing after all.

At the present time we are constantly being brain-washed with the idea that no one is important except as a citizen of the country as a whole, except as a member of a union or of the CBI. Statistics and balance sheets are being offered in place of character. Big Brother is doing his best to smother individuals under great blankets of bureaucracy. Resting on our shoulders in Scotland are community councils, district councils, regional councils, a Scottish Assembly, a Parliament in London and yet another Parliament in Brussels. The mind even of a spiritual Atlas would boggle at the concept. Is it not time to argue that no individual can ever be a good citizen of the country as a whole – or, indeed, of the world – without first being a good citizen of his own parish?

When the Royal Scots Fusiliers stormed ashore in Sicily, officers and men fought and died for their regiment, only incidentally for the British Army. We were the 'Fusil Jocks', Marlborough's Own, not an obscure unit in the 5th Division of the 13th Corps. People like St Columba and St Margaret, Wallace and Bruce and the ladies of the Covenant, Robert Burns, Sir Walter Scott, David Livingstone: all those have left behind examples of nobility to the world, not because they were neatly docketed citizens of the world but because they were independent individuals, ready to sacrifice wealth and comfort, even their very lives, to uphold the values of freedom and the freedom of thought so dear to them as Scots.

A Water Board office shines with chromium. Splendid. But don't let us forget that Water Board machinery is merely the extension of a basic principle. Why allow the parish pump to lie rusty and neglected?

In forty-five years as a free-lance writer in Scotland I have had good times and bad, like any other man. But fortune was with me at the beginning in that it was much easier for an apprentice author to get a book published in 1932 than it is in 1977, when financial considerations inhibit a publisher from taking too many risks. During the middle years it was again fortune – and a kindly BBC – which enabled me to earn what for Jean and me was a satisfactory income. Now, in the old age pension period, fortune still has a smile for me: my books sell in respectable numbers; I am happy with Jean and Jock and friendly with all the other members of the family; I live in the bright open spaces of Southend among kind neighbours who, on the whole, are interested in human rather than material values; I have time to write, to attend church and do my duty as an elder, to play golf, work in the garden and take part in amateur drama.

Being a member of a vital community is one privilege I would never barter, even for a block-busting bestseller. Within the past three years two things have happened to illustrate what I mean.

The first occurred on Sunday 9 June 1974 when, with the co-operation of almost everybody in the parish, including our go-getting young minister, John Russell, and his wife Sheila, and with the technical assistance of Parkin Raine from Barnard Castle and Les Hutchines from London – two BBC engineers who have become adopted Southenders – the *Pageant of St Columba* was presented at the Footsteps at Keil. I had written and produced it, at rehearsals shouting through a megaphone at a cast of over sixty like a Scottish Cecil B. de Mille.

That Sunday morning the weather was bad. Hail showers blew in from the west. But at two o'clock, when the pageant was due to begin, the sun shone on a thousand spectators marshalled on the rock-strewn turf of 'the shoulder of the congregation' by my farming neighbours, Archie Barbour and Robert Ferguson.

Recorded bells rang out, disturbing the gulls on the high cliffs. Manned by Archie Cameron and coastguards Peter Webb and Donald Toon, the coracle appeared in the bay and approached the dark rocks and undulating seaweed on the shore. Meanwhile a pagan procession led by a Druid – retired tailor's assistant Ian Carruthers – began moving towards the Footsteps. There was no more I could do, so I sat there on the edge of the crowd and watched, worrying at first that hitches might rear up like spitting snakes but, when none appeared, becoming more and more conscious of my good luck in being one of such a dedicated and competent team.

I heard Jean's nephew, school-master John McKerral, reading the narration. I watched the players: Andy Dunn, also a school-master, as Briochan, the Archdruid; my golfing 'buddy' Allan Lamont, a retired headmaster, as Gabran, Chief Elect of the Epidii; Agnes McIntyre, the local school-mistress, as his wife and young Robert Ferguson as his infant son. They gathered on the grassy knoll accompanied by male and female servants and by the children of the tribe.

The children played and moved like experienced actors, their faces wrapt and angelic. None of the admiring spectators realized that at one stage during rehearsals, when their behaviour had been less than pacific, I had threatened to throw every scoundrelly one of them over the edge of the cliffs.

I heard the sound of a bugle – a medieval bugle brought all the way from Yorkshire by Harry Hodgson, another adopted Southender. Pert and pretty school-girl Anne McSporran, aged ten, called out that strangers were coming.

Up from the beach strode the singing disciples, at their head Columba, played by Alastair Cousin, the handsome local vet. Two pagan guards armed with spears – burly farmers Donald MacCallum and Ralph Davidson – stopped them at the foot of the knoll, then, reassured, allowed them to pass. I watched the confrontation of the pagan chief and the Christian chief and, later, the baptism of Gabran's son at St Columba's Well.

During it all I listened to the singing organized by Cissie MacConnachie, a farmer's wife, and Hamish Buchanan of the Muneroy Stores. I saw the colourful costumes made by Jan Carruthers and her three assistants and the shepherds' crooks and soldiers' spears whittled into shape by George Cammish and his coastguards. It was team-work by amateurs in the original sense of the word.

At the end Columba and his disciples said farewell to Gabran and moved away along the rocky path. The coracle became a motor-boat again, speeding back towards the jetty at Dunaverty. The whole congregation stood up, and together we sang 'Amazing Grace'.

I was glad that neither film nor television cameras were there and that no professional recording was made for radio. This was a show for Southend by Southenders. It was done in the way we wanted to do it, without interference from audience researchers or chartered accountants. I believe it gave us all a sense of fulfilment.

I remember with pleasure the willingness of everybody to take part.

Alec Harvey is big and hefty, with a ruddy complexion and black curling hair, who works by day as a tractor-man and on clear summer evenings as a casual fencer, painter and chimney-sweep. Sometimes he cuts Jean's drying-green with his rotary mower, and it was on one of these occasions that I approached him to play a disciple. Alec isn't a particularly enthusiastic churchman, but, being part Irish, he looked the part, and I was sure he would be a conscientious attender of rehearsals.

At first he demurred. 'Me, a disciple? The biggest heathen in Soothen'! It's no' possible!'

But when he had finished cutting the grass I put the idea to him again. This time, to my delight, he agreed. 'Great, Alec,' I said. 'I know you're going to enjoy it.'

He looked at me in silence, then shook his head. 'Man, Angus,' he replied, in a lugubrious tone which failed to camouflage a twinkle in his bright eyes, 'ye'll ha'e me walkin' on the watter next!'

During rehearsals, one of the disciples took sick and I asked Alastair Maiden, my friend, near neighbour and the Southend doctor, if he would take his place. At once he, too, agreed to help, though he was anxious about the short time available to practise some movement and mime. 'Follow Alec,' I told him. 'Do as he does and you won't go far wrong.'

When apprised of the situation, Alec was 'fair chuffed'. 'Imagine me tellin' the doctor whit tae dae! I'll get the sack frae ma union if they fin' oot. Demarcation o' areas, ye ken!'

In the outcome they both made outstanding disciples. Alec chose to be bright and breezy, smiling and waving to the 'gallery' as he passed by. Alastair was staid and 'holy', head bent as if in prayer, folded hands hidden in the voluminous sleeves of his habit. Columba himself would have been proud of them.

In the course of the pageant Columba and his disciples were due to walk in procession from the shore to the knoll of the Footsteps. Of necessity, part of this walk had to be along the main road, and I asked the police in Campbeltown for assistance and advice.

'Can the road be closed for half an hour or so?'

My friend Sergeant Hector McKinnon, a native of Tiree, slowly shook his head. 'I'm afraid not. Closing a public highway is just not on, except, of course, if there's an accident or anything like that. And I'm sure you'll not be wanting any accident on Sunday.'

'It's going to be a bit awkward if cars or buses come barging into the procession. For one thing it could be dangerous. For another it would spoil the illusion that the whole thing is taking place fourteen hundred years ago.'

He smiled with Hebridean wisdom. 'Don't worry. I'll put men on the road on either side of the Footsteps. If anybody is bad mannered enough to want to go through, we'll tell them there's a wee hold-up on ahead and ask if they'll please have patience for a minute or two. They'll start watching the pageant and before they realize what's happening it will all be over.'

Hector was as good as his word. Not a single vehicle was seen on the road during the whole of the pageant. The tact and discretion of Scottish policemen – especially if they have Highland connections, as so many of them do – are of a high standard.

Almost as soon as the pageant was finished, the rain and the hail came down again. As we cleared away the fences and the brushwood from around the main stage we all got soaked to the skin. But that didn't worry us. I remember thinking what remarkable progress had occurred in human relationships in Southend during the 300 years since the blood-stained siege of Dunaverty.

The other great moment of my life in a civilized community took place in Campbeltown on Saturday 26 April 1975.

Since 1952 our amateur drama team in Southend, now called the Dunaverty Players, has been competing annually in the SCDA's One Act Play Festival, with varying fortunes. Along the road we have met with happy success and unhappy failure. Up till 1975 we had won the local preliminary festival in Kintyre many times. Only once, however, in 1967, had we reached the Scottish final. That year it was held in the Queen's

Hall, Dunoon, and our intimate little play was lost on the huge stage. But we had kept on trying, because we believed that competitive festivals provided the flow of adrenalin necessary for good performance.

Amateur drama is like war. There are the long periods of training during rehearsals, the sudden bursts of action at festivals, the spit and polish before local shows, the wonderful sensation, at the season's end, of going on leave. I have had more than a quarter of a century of it now, and not one moment would I have missed, even though, like other people involved, it has cost me plenty in time and money.

Why do we do it?

One reason, I think, is that amateur drama provides a means of self-expression – and thus of communicating with other people – denied to football fans and watchers of the telly. Football fans can throw bottles or go 'streaking' across pitches, telly-watchers can blaspheme and kick in their sets when a programme displeases them; but policemen and hire-purchase agents are inclined to frown on such ego-trips. It is safer and more satisfying to take part, to get rid of inhibitions and simmering moral messages by acting them out on the stage for the benefit of audiences.

Another reason is that members of a drama club, working together, can acquire a knowledge of human nature far more extensive than that of people less involved in the social situation. They acquire it in the study of plays, in the discipline necessary to understand and portray the characters in these plays, in the tolerance necessary when a discovery is made (sometimes happy, sometimes sad) of one another. In drama, as in war, team-work is a prerequisite of success. Without discipline, without tolerance there is no team-work. But with discipline and tolerance there is not only team-work but also an end-product of lasting comradeship.

On account of our geographical situation we in Southend have seldom the opportunity of measuring our productions against those in the professional theatre. (There is television theatre, of course; but though valuable as a guide to characterization this has little to offer the stage as far as plot, movement and projection are concerned.) As far as possible, however, we have tried to maintain high standards, and through the SCDA's advisers, travelling the countryside in wind, rain and snow (like our own club members), we have learned, slowly but surely, what these standards are. Occasionally we have approached attainment. More often we fail, but this is our fault, not that of the advisers.

Through the years we have also learned that amateur drama is not designed for our pleasure alone. We have recognized that the theatre was invented for the benefit of the populace, not for self-indulgent actors and producers, and that artistic achievement depends on the willing co-operation of an audience. There is nothing sadder, for me, than the yawning apathy from 'front of house' when certain 'experimental' plays are being dragged out on stage, but nothing more wonderful than the response of an audience which gives utter silence during a moment of tension then laughs uproariously when the playwright and his actors change the mood.

At the beginning of the 1974–5 season, therefore, we in the Dunaverty Players had considerable knowledge behind us, even though we do live at the Mull of Kintyre and the population of Southend is only 500. A play was chosen called *Rise and Shine*, by a Canadian writer, Elda Cadogan. Set in a graveyard, like many good plays it didn't look particularly promising at first; but the comedy was sharp and the plot appealed to our Scottish sense of humour, which can discover fun even in funerals.

Alastair Maiden, fresh from his stint as a disciple, took over production. He recruited Hamish Buchanan as stage manager; Margaret Cameron, assistant in a local shop, as prompter; Jan Carruthers as wardrobe mistress and Parkin Raine as effects man. (One of the effects was the Last Trump, so a BBC engineer was needed to cope with that one.) Jim Johnstone, manager of an ink factory, was made leading man and Jennifer, John McKerral's American wife, leading lady. Mabel Maiden,

Alastair's wife, and John McKerral himself, our most experienced actor, were given the two supporting parts.

Rehearsals were occasionally fraught, as the cast struggled with Canadian accents. The stage crew, which included Jim Johnstone's wife Maureen, farmer's daughter Janet Ferguson and Jan Carruthers' husband Ian, laboured to produce polystyrene tombstones and to paint them in mouldering shades of green and grey. But at the preliminary SCDA festival in Campbeltown *Rise and Shine* was a clear winner with both the adjudicator and the audience. (Strange as it may seem, this happy conjunction doesn't always occur.)

Our next move was to the SCDA Western Divisional Final in Castle Douglas. As we were due to perform on a Saturday evening we hired a bus and, after our work, began the journey late on the Friday afternoon. The bus-driver was young Jim Cameron, who understands about temperamental 'dramatists' and who, during our long-distance forays, regards himself as one of the team. Unfortunately, when we reached a certain roundabout near Ayr, Jim received bad advice from somebody and took the wrong road. As midnight approached we found ourselves near Sanquhar, lost in a country of heather and streaming rain and apparently as far away from Castle Douglas as we had been hours before.

The trouble was, nobody had remembered to bring a map. A committee formed itself to decide on a valid route. But as so often happens with committees its members could find no point of agreement. Through the darkness – 'through the night of doubt and sorrow' – we thundered on, following tracks which plunged down into glens and reared up across bare hills, arguments raging in the committee as we came to unidentified road-forks and junctions.

That night, in many a remote hamlet in Dumfries-shire and Kirkcudbrightshire, I am sure legends were born of a ghost bus passing through on its way to the afterworld; and if the uneasy inhabitants had chanced to glimpse the pile of tombstones and other graveyard props at the back of Jim's bus, their supernatural fears would have been confirmed. (There was one small village which, inadvertently, we encountered twice, another which heard the swishing and squelching of our tyres three times.)

At last, however, somewhere near New Galloway, we came upon a sign: 'Castle Douglas – 8 miles'. We were saved.

It was after one o'clock in the morning when we reached our hotel. Having arrived hours before by car, Jock and Parkin Raine were there to welcome us and prescribe soothing 'medicine'. Our ordeal was soon forgotten.

And forgotten so thoroughly that on the following evening *Rise and Shine* won the Divisional Cup, and we found ourselves – incredibly – moving forward to the Scottish final, with teams from Paisley, Greenock and Glasgow floundering in our wake.

While the adjudicator was making his final remarks I sat with Jim Johnstone, who had wiped off his greasepaint and made a hurried change from costume into conventional garb. As the result was announced we sprang to our feet, embraced each other and let out a simultaneous roar, like the roar of steam escaping from over-stressed boilers. All the hard work, all the frustrations and anxieties were forgotten in a moment of sheer delight. People around us laughed. What did we care?

Producer Alastair came on stage to receive the trophy. I could see that he was in a daze of glory, hardly conscious of what was happening. Tomorrow he would realize that in less than a month he would be faced with the problem of whipping his team back into action for the Scottish Final at Campbeltown. As for me, I was beginning to believe that a vision which had inspired the Dunaverty Players for almost twenty-five years might be verging on reality.

Campbeltown's Victoria Hall being our home ground, it was like Rangers playing the final of the SFA Cup at Ibrox or Celtic playing it at Parkhead. There are advantages in such a situation: the home team has no long-distance travelling to do and the 'ground staff' are sympathetic. There is also one disadvantage:

the home team becomes so anxious to do well before a local audience that pressure builds up to a dangerous level.

During that beautiful April evening, as we prepared to stage the most important performance in our history, temperaments bubbled. I dared not approach members of the team even to wish them well. Alastair, usually so kind and gentle, growled like a cornered bear. Hamish Buchanan lost his 'behind the counter' charm and snapped angrily at anybody who went near his precious tombstones. Jim Johnstone could not eat, drink or speak. Jennifer McKerral threw tantrums at Jan Carruthers about her stage 'goonie'. Mabel Maiden looked as grim as the black, Presbyterian character she was about to portray. John McKerral, old trouper though he was, kept repeating his lines and declaring that he was about to forget them all.

When the curtain went up on *Rise and Shine* I found myself sitting among the audience in a state of tension equalled only twice before in my life: first, when Jock was born, and second, when I faced a television camera for the first time. Jean was so tense herself that she had no comfort to spare. Jock, beside us, tried hard to achieve a sports reporter's blasé objectivity, but his silence betrayed him. Around us, all the Dunaverty Players not taking part were biting finger-nails and composing silent, incoherent prayers.

Soon after the performance began, I sensed that a terrible thing was happening. At the preliminary festival in the same hall, the Kintyre audience had laughed without inhibitions; now it was afraid to laugh, in case laughter might upset the players. When an audience responds actors blossom like flowers in June sunlight. When it is restrained, worrying more about the performance than the play, actors feel it and tend to strain for effect. But as *Rise and Shine* went on I began to see the value of persistent rehearsals. The players were living on the substance of what they had learned and practised. In spite of their nerves they were doing well. Not so well as at Castle Douglas, where laughter and applause had lifted their spirits, but well enough.

Afterwards, Alastair and his actors were despondent. They felt they had done badly and could not be persuaded that instinctive skill had brought success.

At the end of the festival, when the adjudicator came on stage to announce the final placings, I knew from 'a gut reaction' (to flourish a fashionable phrase) that the winner must be either Paisley Old Grammarians with *Plaza Suite, Act III* or Dunaverty Players with *Rise and Shine*. And when first place was given to Dunaverty Players – and second to Paisley Old Grammarians – with 600 others in the Victoria Hall I rose to my feet and gave a long shout of triumph. It was hard to believe. We were Scottish champions.

I went on stage to congratulate Alastair. He was clutching the cup in the zombiefied way a pools winner clutches a six-figure cheque. I put out my hand. He saw it and put out his. But he walked past me, his hand still outstretched, and became tangled with the stage drapes. At that moment he was the leading amateur producer in Scotland. No wonder he had contracted what he himself might have diagnosed as 'euphoric trauma'.

That was a night, that was. Mary Taylor, the club president, decreed that joy should be 'unconfined'. At one stage I sang a song in praise of the producer. I called it 'The Gentle Maiden', but the words bore no resemblance to those of the original. I felt like a Sisyphus, who, miraculously, has at last got his block of marble to the top of the hill.

Perhaps it wouldn't stay up there for long. In that case there would be no regrets.

After all, hill-tops are draughty places.

Index

BESTSELLERS FROM ARROW

All these books are available from your bookshop or newsagent or you can order them direct. Just tick the titles you want and complete the form below.

A CHOICE OF CATASTROPHIES	Isaac Asimov	£1.95
BRUACH BLEND	Lillian Beckwith	95p
THE HISTORY MAN	Malcolm Bradbury	£1.60
A LITTLE ZIT ON THE SIDE	Jasper Carrott	£1.25
EENY MEENY MINEY MOLE	Marcel A'Agneau	£1.50
HERO	Leslie Deane	£1.75
TRAVELS WITH FORTUNE	Christine Dodwell	£1.50
11th ARROW BOOK OF CROSSWORDS	Frank Henchard	95p
THE LOW CALORIE MENU BOOK	Joyce Hughes	90p
THE PALMISTRY OF LOVE	David Brandon-Jones	£1.50
DEATH DREAMS	William Katz	£1.25
PASSAGE TO MUTINY	Alexander Kent	£1.50
HEARTSOUNDS	Marth Weinman Lear	£1.75
LOOSELY ENGAGED	Christopher Matthew	£1.25
HARLOT	Margaret Pemberton	£1.60
TALES FROM A LONG ROOM	Peter Tinniswood	£1.50
INCIDENT ON ATH	E. C. Tubb	£1.15
THE SECOND LADY	Irving Wallace	£1.75
STAND BY YOUR MAN	Tammy Wynette	£1.75
DEATH ON ACCOUNT	Margaret Yorke	£1.00
	Postage	————
	Total	————

ARROW BOOKS, BOOKSERVICE BY POST, PO BOX 29, DOUGLAS, ISLE OF MAN, BRITISH ISLES

Please enclose a cheque or postal order made out to Arrow Books Limited for the amount due including 10p per book for postage and packing for orders within the UK and 12p for overseas orders.

Please print clearly

NAME ....

ADDRESS..

....

Whilst every effort is made to keep prices down and to keep popular books in print, Arrow Books cannot guarantee that prices will be the same as those advertised here or that the books will be available.